D1564132

Student Handbook to Economics

Microeconomics

Volume I

Student Handbook to Economics

Microeconomics

Volume I

JULIA A. HEATH

Facts On File
An Infobase Learning Company

Student Handbook to Economics: Microeconomics
Copyright © 2013 Julia A. Heath

Facts On File, Inc.
An Imprint of Infobase Learning
132 West 31st Street
New York NY 10001

Library of Congress Cataloging-in-Publication Data
Student handbook to economics.
    v. cm.
  Includes bibliographical references and index.
  Contents: v. 1. Microeconomics / Julia A. Heath — v. 2. Macroeconomics / Jane S. Lopus — v. 3. International economics / Jane S. Lopus — v. 4. History of economic thought / David Bourne — v. 5. Entrepreneurship / William Smith.
  ISBN 978-1-60413-992-1 (alk. paper) — ISBN 978-1-60413-994-5 (alk. paper) — ISBN 978-1-60413-993-8 (alk. paper) — ISBN 978-1-60413-995-2 (alk. paper) — ISBN 978-1-60413-996-9 (alk. paper) — ISBN 978-1-60413-997-6 (alk. paper) 1. Economics—Handbooks, manuals, etc. 2. Microeconomics—Handbooks, manuals, etc. 3. Macroeconomics—Handbooks, manuals, etc. 4. International economic relations—Handbooks, manuals, etc. 5. Entrepreneurship—Handbooks, manuals, etc. I. Heath, Julia A.
  HB171.5.S9247 2012
  330—dc23
                    2012019189

Facts On File books are available at special discounts when purchased in bulk quantities for businesses, associations, institutions, or sales promotions. Please call our Special Sales Department in New York at (212) 967-8800 or (800) 322-8755.

You can find Facts On File on the World Wide Web at http://www.infobaselearning.com

Text design by Erika K. Arroyo
Cover design by Takeshi Takahashi
Composition by EJB Publishing Services
Cover printed by Yurchak Printing, Landisville, Pa.
Book printed and bound by Yurchak Printing, Landisville, Pa.
Printed in the United States of America

This book is printed on acid-free paper.

CONTENTS

What is economics? Even if you do not have a clear definition of economics in mind, you probably have some good ideas regarding what economics is all about. On a personal level, you know that economics involves jobs and income and whether you can afford to buy things that you want. If you are running a business or plan to do so, economics involves concerns such as costs, revenues, profits, and how to start or expand your business. On a national level, economics looks at issues such as the overall levels of prices, unemployment, and economic growth. Economics also involves international issues such as trade and exchange rates. Some people are under the impression that economics is only about the study of money. Economists do study money, but economics includes much more than this.

The basic economic problem is scarcity. Scarcity exists because economic resources are limited, but people's wants are not. Because of scarcity, we cannot have all of the goods and services that we would like for ourselves and for others, and therefore we have to make choices. Economics is very much about making choices and deciding how to make the best use of scarce resources. With this in mind, we can define economics as a social science concerned with the way society chooses to use its scarce resources to produce goods and services to satisfy people's wants.

The five volumes in our series *Student Handbook to Economics* provide a solid foundation for learning about major topics related to economics and for learning about different approaches to studying economics. *Microeconomics* looks at economics from the viewpoint of individuals, businesses, or industries. It involves studying about supply and demand, or how prices are established in a market economic system. What role the government should play when markets do not work perfectly is another important microeconomic topic.

Macroeconomics looks at economics from the perspective of the whole economy. Macroeconomics addresses problems such as inflation, unemployment, and why the economy has its ups and downs. Macroeconomics also addresses what the government and central bank can try to do about problems in the economy. Our *International Economics* volume investigates topics such as globalization, economic development, trade and trade barriers, exchange rates, and different types of economic systems.

The fourth volume in our economics series, *History of Economic Thought,* takes a historical perspective and traces economic philosophy from Aristotle to the present, addressing the interesting and important topic of the philosophies underlying various economic theories. The fifth volume in our series, *Entrepreneurship,* focuses on the innovative business side of economics. What are the types of business organizations? What is the role of market research? How can you create a company or expand a company? Each of the five volumes provides a framework for better understanding economic topics and issues.

Why is it important to study economics? It is important because it will help you to make better decisions on a personal level. With a better understanding of the world around you, you will be able to make better choices as a consumer and producer or entrepreneur. You will have a better understanding of local, national, and international events and trends covered by the media. You will become a more informed participant in our democracy, and a more informed participant in our global economy. We wish you the best as you embark on your exciting adventure.

## CHAPTER 1

WHAT IS MICROECONOMICS?

INTRODUCTION

The subject of this book is microeconomics, one of several subfields in the discipline of economics. One goal of this book is to familiarize you with this aspect of economics; another goal is to show you that virtually everything around you has something to do with microeconomics—even baseball. In 1915, the Boston Red Sox had a left-handed pitcher who dominated the league. He led the team to World Series titles in 1916 and 1918. In 1916, he set a record for most consecutive scoreless innings that lasted until 1961. In 1919, he was traded to another team where he was put in the outfield and pitched only 17 more games. Do you know who this player was? And why, given that he was such a talented pitcher, would his new team not have him pitch?

The answer to the first question is Babe Ruth. The answer to the second question has to do with microeconomics and will be revealed later in this chapter.

MICROECONOMICS VS. MACROECONOMICS

Before we follow up on our baseball story, we need to differentiate between **microeconomics** and **macroeconomics**. Macroeconomics is the study of the "big picture"—the nation's unemployment rate, policies of the Federal Reserve Bank, the government's fiscal policies. All of us are significantly affected by macroeconomic conditions and government and Fed reactions to them. The basics of macroeconomics are explained in Volume II of this series. This volume is about microeconomics—the "little picture."

Although we are all affected by what happens at the macro level, we have little control over the workings of the larger economy (except through our voting behavior). In contrast, we all live microeconomics every day. As we go through each day, we continuously apply concepts from microeconomics, even though we do so without consciously recognizing it. At its most fundamental level, microeconomics is about making decisions—consumer decisions, business decisions, and some government decisions. All of this decision making is necessary because there is a scarcity of the things that we want. If there were an infinite supply of resources and time, we would not have to make any choices—we could have it all! Because of scarcity, we have to choose. Microeconomics is about how consumers, businesses, and governments make economic decisions within various contexts, even though the motivation for each person, institution, and entity may be different. For example, businesses make decisions about the price of their output depending upon what kind of competitive environment they operate in. Consumers decide whether to buy something or not depending on the price of the desired good, other prices, and a host of other factors. Governments decide whether to levy a tax on a good after examining how sensitive consumers are to the price of that good.

As we go through this volume, we will explore different contexts and discuss how changing a situation alters the decisions of consumers, businesses, and governments. But what remains constant is that whatever the context, a decision must be made. Let's take a closer look at decision making and at how economics frames the process of choosing. You might think that making an economic decision is fairly easy and certainly doesn't require a whole section of a book (or an entire discipline) to explain how to do it correctly. You would be wrong. Making an economic decision (a good one, anyway) is a complicated process consisting of several interrelated components.

MAKING A DECISION: THE CONSEQUENCES

The most basic part of making a decision actually involves looking at the thing that is not chosen. When you make a choice, you give something up. Every time. What you give up is the thing you did not choose. This is called the **opportunity cost** of your decision. The opportunity cost is the next best alternative—the runner-up—to what you did choose. Thus if you are trying to decide between going to the movies with friends and staying in to do homework, whichever decision you make incurs a cost. Suppose you choose to go the movies. You have to buy the ticket (and popcorn, etc.) and you have to drive to the theater (using gasoline), but you also have incurred an opportunity cost (not doing your homework). Suppose you decide to stay in to do your homework instead. You may think that you have incurred no cost at all—after all, working on your history homework doesn't cost you anything! But it does—the cost of doing your homework is giving up the fun you would have had by going to the movies with your friends.

Now let's add a third choice to this mix. Suppose you had to decide between going to the movies, doing your homework, and visiting your grandmother. If you decide to go to the movies, your opportunity cost is your next best alternative, not both of the remaining alternatives. So, if you choose to go to the movies and your second choice is visiting your grandmother, only the visit is your opportunity cost, not visiting your grandmother <u>and</u> doing your homework. No matter how many alternatives you are choosing from, only one of them—your second best option—is your opportunity cost. A simple way to think about opportunity cost is to ask yourself, "What am I giving up?"

Knowing what your opportunity cost is makes it possible for you to make better choices. Unless you can articulate what a particular choice will cost you (all of the costs), you cannot make a fully informed decision. Assume that you are on the fence about going to college—maybe it is right for you, but you are just not sure. Maybe getting a job right out of high school is a better choice. Let's look at the costs for both options.

As you can see, the costs of going to college include direct costs (tuition and books), but also include the opportunity cost of lost wages for four years. Likewise, getting a job immediately after high school has some direct costs associated with it, but also has opportunity costs, including the potential loss of higher wages over your working life. Which of these costs is higher is a matter for you to estimate, but the important part here is to include all of the costs for both options.

Remember our question about the left-handed pitching sensation Babe Ruth? He was an outstanding pitcher for the Red Sox, but when he was traded in 1919, he rarely pitched again. The reason he rarely pitched again is because the opportunity cost for him to do so for his new team (the Yankees) would

TABLE 1.1
Comparing the Costs

Your Choices and Your Costs	
Going to College	**Going to Work**
• Tuition and fees • Room and board • Books • Wages you could have earned for 4 years if you had worked	• Room and board • Will probably need a car • Missing out on social aspects of college • Higher lifetime earnings of a college grad compared to a high school grad

have been too high. If the Yankees had played him as a pitcher, they would have incurred a cost—the other position he could have played. For the Yankees, Ruth was more valuable in the outfield, playing (and hitting) every day. Pitching meant he would not have played every day.

MAKING A DECISION: WHY COMPLETE INFORMATION MATTERS

Thinking through the consequences (opportunity costs) of a decision is all well and good, but in order to do that, you need to have enough information to make your decision a reasonably good one. So how much information is enough information? The section title includes the word "complete." In the real world, however, we rarely have all the information that is potentially available before we make a decision. So, in this context, "complete" does not mean every single bit of information—it means enough for you to make a reasonable choice.

Although complete information is desirable, in most cases we don't have it. Nonetheless, we make decisions even when some information is missing. For example, if you are in the market for a used car, the seller will always have more information about the true condition of the car than you have. As a buyer, you are aware of this asymmetry of information and know that you will have trouble telling the good cars from the so-so cars. Let's assume that you are willing to pay $10,000 for a good, used car, but only $5,000 for a so-so one. You assume that half of the used cars out there are good and the other half are so-so. You find a car that you are interested in and make an offer of $7,500. This seems like a fair offer to you because you have a 50-50 chance of getting a good car (or a so-so one), and you just split the difference between what each car is worth to you (.5 × $10,000 + .5 × $5,000 = $7,500). Will the seller of the car be willing to accept your $7,500 offer? If he or she is selling a good car, your offer will not be accepted because good cars are worth $10,000. If the seller accepts your offer, he or she must be selling a so-so car, and you are paying $2,500 more than what that car is actually worth to you. The only cars that will be sold in this kind of market are the less-than-desirable ones, an outcome called **adverse selection**. In an effort to give you more information, used car dealers can offer warranties, or you can get a CarFax® report or take the car to a mechanic before you buy it. Used car dealers can also attempt to build a reputation for selling high-quality used cars in an effort to minimize the adverse selection problem.

Adverse selection can also occur when the buyer has more information than the seller. In the market for insurance, for example, the person buying the insurance often has more information about him- or herself than the insurance company does. In the automobile insurance market, for example, you know more about your driving habits (and how risky they are) than the insurance company does. In fact, the riskier a driver you are, the more likely it is that you will want insurance. If this were the only criterion, the market for auto insurance would be dominated by risky drivers. In the real world, however, most

Babe Ruth and opportunity costs. The Red Sox pitching sensation rarely pitched for the New York Yankees because he was more valuable playing in the outfield every day.

states require all drivers to have auto insurance. With this requirement, the market for insurance is expanded beyond risky drivers to include everyone.

Asymmetric information can interfere with making good decisions. Although you cannot completely eliminate asymmetric information before making a choice about something, you can take steps to minimize its effects. Being aware that this kind of information exists is the most important, first step. As a buyer, you can then do the appropriate research to gather more information about the product, the seller, or both. You can do this research through the Better Business Bureau, through product ratings (such as those provided by Consumer Reports), and through general Internet searches. The same principle holds true if you are a seller.

MAKING A DECISION: WHAT NOT TO CONSIDER

Have you ever gone to a movie and discovered about half-way through it, that it is an awful movie? Not just a movie that is so-so, but one that is truly awful? What did you do? Did you get up and walk out? Or did you stay through to the end, thinking, "I've already paid for it, I might as well stay"? If you stayed, you used the concept of **sunk costs** in your decision. A lot of people do this—and they shouldn't.

Sunk costs are costs that you incurred in the past that you cannot get back. They should not be used in deciding what to do going forward. Those costs are gone, and regardless of what you do from this point forward, that won't change. Let's revisit the movie example. You have already paid for your ticket. If you do not like the movie, you cannot get your money back—it is a sunk cost. So, how do you decide if you should stay and watch the rest of the movie or leave? You should base your decision on factors that exist in the present, not in the past. Balance the benefits of leaving (e.g., you can use the time to do something else) against the costs of leaving (you might be embarrassed). Likewise, you should balance the potential benefits of staying (maybe the movie will get better?) against the costs of staying (further annoyance and the opportunity cost of your time). What you should not consider is the cost of your ticket because regardless of what you do—stay or leave—you cannot get that money back. You paid in the past and that cannot be changed.

It can be very difficult psychologically to ignore sunk costs in decision making. They represent money or time that has been invested, and walking away from them (physically or mentally) is very hard to do and often feels wasteful. But in dwelling on sunk costs, you are continuing to direct resources into some activity just because you have already invested in it. And this is wasteful and not good decision making. To illustrate this, let's consider two new scenarios:

Scenario 1: You are on your way to see one of your favorite bands perform. The cover charge is $10. When you get there, you realize that somewhere along the way, a $10 bill fell out of your pocket. You still have another $10 to pay the cover.

Scenario 2: You have purchased the cover wristband for your favorite band ahead of time—it cost you $10. When you get there, you discover that somehow the wrist band has fallen off your wrist and you can't get in. You can purchase another wristband at the door for $10.

What would you do in the first scenario? What would you do in the second scenario? Does your decision depend on whether you had already paid the money or not? A good decision in either case has nothing to do with paying or not paying the $10. It has everything to do with whether you think it's worth it to pay $10. In each case, the question you ask yourself and the answer to that question should be the same: Is it worth $10 to me to see this band?"

In Scenario 1, you were willing to buy a ticket for $10 so you probably thought seeing the band was worth $10. The fact that $10 fell out of your pocket shouldn't enter into this equation. Seeing the band still costs you $10. In Scenario 2, you already purchased a $10 wristband to see the band. If you pay again, you may feel that you are actually paying $20 to see the band play. But the lost wristband cannot be part of the equation because it is a sunk cost—you cannot recover it. If you don't buy another wristband, you won't get your lost money back. If you buy another wristband, the price of seeing the band will still be $10.

The important point here is that the decision to see the band or not see the band in each of these scenarios is neither right or wrong. The decision you make should be the same in both cases—if losing your wristband means that you wouldn't buy another one, then you also should not be willing to spend $10 if you lost your money on the way. Above all, the decision is about going forward and not factoring in something that has already happened and cannot be undone.

So, the next time you find yourself in a situation where you are thinking, "I've already spent my money (or time, or any other resource) on this, I might as well . . . "—step back and ask yourself if you are dealing with a sunk cost. Can you recover the resource that is already spent? If not, then do not consider what you've already invested. Ask yourself what options are available to you from this point forward. In other words, is it worth the $10 or $100 or $1,000 right now?

MAKING A DECISION: IT'S ALL MARGINAL

In popular usage, if we say something is "marginal," it usually means that it's not very good. But with economics, a marginal decision is exactly the kind of decision you want to make.

Making decisions at the margin means that you consider the costs and benefits of spending one more—dollar, hour, or whatever, depending on what the situation is. Let's assume that you are on the track team and are trying to decide how much time you should devote to training. You want to improve your time, but recognize that if you devote more time to training, you will need to give

TABLE 1.2
Making Marginal Decisions

Choices	Benefit	Cost (Opportunity)
Train for extra 30 minutes	Time decreases by 20%	Lost 30 minutes of study time
Train for extra 60 minutes	Time decreases by 30%	Lost 60 minutes of study time
Train for extra 90 minutes	Time decreases by 35%	Lost 90 minutes of study time

something up, like time for studying (opportunity cost). Your trade-off is shown in Table 1.2.

Before looking at making decisions at the margin, let's look at how not to make a decision. You might think that because you can reduce your time by 35 percent if you train for 90 more minutes, that's what you should do. You look at that benefit and compare it to the cost of the loss of 90 minutes of study time and conclude that it's worth it. But that's not a good enough basis for making a decision. Although it is important to weigh the costs and benefits, there is a better way to approach this decision.

According to the table, if you spend an extra 30 minutes training, you can decrease your time by 20 percent. Likewise, if you spend an extra hour training, your time will decrease by 30 percent. But this additional 30 minutes decreases your time by only an additional 10 percentage points (from 20 percent to 30 percent). So the first half-hour results in a benefit of a 20 percent reduction, and the second half-hour results in an additional, or **marginal benefit** of only 10 percent. What does the third half-hour get you? If you train for 90 minutes, you will only gain 5 percent on your time over what your benefit would be if you trained for an hour.

As you can see, the marginal benefit of each additional 30-minute block falls as you increase your training time. This result, **diminishing marginal benefit**, is not unique to this example. It is typical for marginal benefit to fall as the thing you are devoting time and effort to increases. Let's look at another example, one that you may be more familiar with. Perhaps you have a B average for your overall GPA. If you get one more A, your GPA will go up quite a bit. If you get another one, your GPA will increase, but not as much as with the first A. The third A also raises your GPA, but by an even smaller amount than the second one did. By the time you get to your fifth or sixth A, the increase to your GPA is very small.

This declining "bang for your buck" is an important concept to keep in mind when making decisions because it represents a more accurate picture of how much the benefit is actually worth. Remember that the more time or effort you put into training or to getting that sixth A, the more you need to give something else up. In our training example, the opportunity cost of each 30-minute block of training is the same amount of time spent studying. When you increase training time by the first 30 minutes, the cost is 30 minutes of studying. When you increase it by the second 30 minutes, the cost is 30 additional minutes of studying, and so on.

At first glance, the additional, or **marginal cost** of each 30-minute block in the training example stays the same: 30 minutes of studying time. But it is easy to imagine how that might not be the case. If you need more time to stretch and cool down after a long training session (say 90 minutes) than after a shorter one (60 minutes), then you would lose more than 30 minutes of studying time because you would have to spend more time stretching and cooling down. Therefore the marginal cost of that last 30-minute block might actually be 40 minutes of lost studying time.

Just as it is typical for marginal benefit to decline when the activity (training) or entity (GPA) increases, it is common for the marginal cost to increase (or at least stay the same). In order to go from 4 As to 5 As to 6 As, you would probably have to give up increasing amounts of time that you would otherwise spend doing other things. To improve from 4 As to 5 As, you might have to give up three hours a week of hanging out with friends. But to go from 5 As to 6 As, you would have to give up 4 hours a week with your friends. Why? Because you become less efficient at studying and have to put more effort into it the longer you do it. Thus your marginal cost increases.

To make a good decision in each of these cases, you need to weigh the marginal benefits and the marginal costs—not total benefits and total costs. So your track coach may be saying you need to train an additional 90 minutes because it decreases your time by 35 percent. But the appropriate way to look at this is in increments. Is it worth it to you, in terms of what you have to give up, to increase your training time by 30 minutes? Because the return is so big (20 percent reduction in time) compared to losing 30 minutes of study time, you might conclude that it is worth it. What about increasing your time by 60 minutes? Your gain of 10 percent (over an extra 30 minutes) has to be compared to your loss of another 30 minutes of studying time. So you compare a 10 percent marginal benefit with a 30 minute loss of study time. Is that worth it? Finally, should you increase your training by 90 minutes? Your marginal benefit is only 5 percent, (over an extra 60 minutes) compared to a loss of 30 (or more) minutes of studying. Your track coach may not like it, but this 5 percent improvement in your time may not be worth it.

Likewise, your GPA can improve with additional studying, but is each addition to your GPA worth it? Rather than asking yourself if a 3.9 GPA is worth giving up 4 hours with your friends every week, you should look at the marginal benefits. For example, is going from a 3.89 to a 3.9 worth one more hour spent with friends (or doing anything else)? Again, your parents may not like it, but when you look at marginal increases instead of at the total, sometimes those marginal costs outweigh the marginal benefits.

SUMMARY

Microeconomics is about how individuals and businesses make decisions. In this chapter we have covered the basics of decision making. Making appropriate decisions, means considering opportunity costs—what is being given up? Making a fully informed decision means understanding and addressing asymmetric information. Sunk costs should not be part of the decision-making process because they cannot be recovered. Decisions should be made looking forward, not looking back. Finally, decisions that are made "at the margin" are more sound than those which ignore the fact that benefits fall and costs rise when more of something is done. We will revisit these concepts throughout the rest of the book, both in the context of individual decision making and in exploring decisions made in the business world. These concepts, in fact, are the core of economics.

Further Reading

Arnold, R.A. *How to Think Like an Economist*. Mason, Ohio: South-Western College Publishing, 2004.

Bauman, Y. *A Cartoon Introduction to Microeconomics*. New York: Hill and Wang Publishers, 2010.

Heyne, P., P.J. Boettke, and D.L. Prychitko. *The Economic Way of Thinking*. New York: Prentice Hall, 2009.

Jevons, M. *Murder at the Margin*. Princeton, N.J.: Princeton University Press, 1993.

## CHAPTER 2

DEMAND AND SUPPLY

INTRODUCTION

This chapter is about demand and supply. While it is overly simplistic to summarize the entire discipline of economics with these two words, the fact is that most economic trends and activities can be explained as a result of demand and supply. But demand and supply are not as simple as they sound. So the objective of this chapter is to explain what these terms really mean and how they influence economics throughout the world. Once you understand the basics, demand and supply can answer a wide array of questions that at first glance may seem to have nothing to do with economics. For example, what do demand and supply have to do with brown eggs being more expensive than white eggs? Or with the shortage of organs needed for transplants? A fundamental understanding of the power of demand and supply can provide answers to these and many other "I've always wondered about that" economic questions.

WHERE DO PRICES COME FROM?

Let's say you want to buy a used car. You see an advertisement in the newspaper for a car that seems like it would be perfect for you. So you call the seller and make arrangements to see the car. After you take the car for a test drive, you are more convinced than ever—you want to buy this car! Now it's time to sit down with the seller and try to come to a price that is agreeable to both of you. How do you do that? Because you are the buyer, you think about two things: how much you value the car and how much you can afford to spend on the car. In other words, you think about your willingness and ability to buy the car. The seller is also thinking about two things. The first thing is how willing he is to sell you the car—in other words, what is the **opportunity cost**? After all, someone else might come along and have a higher willingness and ability to pay for the car than you do. So the seller thinks about what is given up if the car is sold to you. The second thing the seller thinks about is getting a high enough price to cover the costs associated with the car. The seller paid something to acquire and maintain the car, but the car has depreciated in value since he bought it. This means that he has to consider the net costs—costs minus depreciation. The bottom line is that the seller wants to get a price that meets or exceeds those net costs.

You and the seller represent two sides of a **market.** A market is simply where buying and selling occur. Sometimes it is a physical location: the seller's kitchen, a farmers' market, the stock market, or a car dealership. At other times, no actual physical location is necessary, like when someone buys something on eBay. In other words, a market exists anywhere one or more buyers and sellers can communicate and exchange goods and services. In our example, the market happens to be someone's kitchen.

The market that exists between you and the seller of the car you want is a very simple one. Now the two of you must agree on a price, so you sit across from one another at the kitchen table and begin the process of getting to that mutually acceptable price. You offer a price, the seller counters with a higher price, and on you go until you reach a price that meets your two criteria (able and willing) and his two criteria (willing and covering costs). At that point, the two of you have established a **market-clearing**, or **equilibrium**, price. An equilibrium price is simply the price that the buyer and seller agree upon. Both you and the seller have gained from this transaction. You have acquired a car that is at least as valuable to you as the money you will pay the seller to get it. The seller gets your money, which more than covers the value of the car (the costs he incurred to buy and maintain the car minus depreciation). Because the exchange is voluntary, you both benefit. In other words, it is a **mutually beneficial exchange**.

It is relatively easy to see how a market works and how prices are determined when the market consists of only two participants. But how does it work when there are more than two—when there are hundreds, or thousands? The short answer is that it works in exactly the same way. The communication between buyers and sellers is more complicated than the dickering you would do in the seller's kitchen, but communication does exist. Let's say you go into a store, wanting to buy a new sweater. You find one that you like (you are willing to buy it), but it costs too much money (you are not able to buy it, or you might actually have the money to buy it but are not willing to buy it at the price shown on the tag.) How do you communicate with the seller that the price is higher than you are willing to pay? In the seller's kitchen, you can say, "The price you're asking is too high, but I would be willing to pay this much." You cannot do that in most stores. You simply don't take the sweater up to the cash register and start negotiating the price with the cashier or with the store's manager or owner. So how do you communicate your feelings about the price to the seller? You walk out of the store without the sweater.

If you are the only one who leaves without buying a sweater, there will be no effect on the price. But if many, many other people come look at the sweater(s) and leave the store without buying, it sends a message: the price is too high. When merchandise does not sell, it sits on the shelves. When it sits there long enough and starts accumulating, it communicates to the seller that something that should be happening is not happening. This is more complex than sitting across the kitchen table from someone and telling that person the price is too high, but it is just as effective.

Now let's go back to the sweater example. Suppose you (and many others) think the price of the sweater you like is very low. Chance are that you (and a lot of those other people who like the sweater) will buy it. In fact, you might actually leave the store with more than one sweater, maybe two or three. This also communicates something to the seller. When merchandise moves quickly (and especially at higher volumes than expected), this communicates to the seller that perhaps the price can be raised a bit. This back and forth communication continues until both sides of the market reach an equilibrium price.

You may be wondering how this wordless communication results in an equilibrium price when the mechanism for communicating is so cumbersome. When you are negotiating with one seller, things move quickly. But with many buyers and many sellers, communication can be slow. What makes the market communication work is that both sides have experience in the market already—neither buyers nor sellers are starting from zero. Buyers have a pretty good idea of what they are able and willing to spend before they go into a store. Sellers have a good idea of what the market will bear, based on their past experiences. So what is really being communicated is any deviation from what normally occurs. For example, if buyers' circumstances have changed, or if sellers have experienced a change in costs, then communication needs to occur to let the other side of the market know about these changes, and consequently, the change in price.

One final word about markets. Markets allow buyers and sellers to come together to agree on the terms of exchange. A market does not have anything to say about whether the exchange "should" happen, or whether the buyer "deserves" the product, or whether the seller "deserves" to make money. Markets have no conscience, so from a market perspective, it does not matter if what is being exchanged is a car or heroin. The market passes no judgment on the exchange or on the participants—it simply provides the means for the exchange to occur.

We will present this information somewhat more formally below, but the basics are exactly the same as what was discussed here. There are two sides in the market for anything: buyers and sellers. Buyers and sellers communicate to establish a market-clearing, or equilibrium price. At this price, every buyer who is able and willing to pay that price, will be able to purchase the item under consideration. This is also the price at which sellers will be able to sell that item (in fact, all individual units of that item) they have for sale.

DEMAND AND SUPPLY ILLUSTRATED

With the basics explained, let's make the discussion of demand and supply a bit more formal by using some graphs. Graphs often help us understand what happens when the market changes much better than words alone. We'll use a fictitious product, Bubbly Pop cola, as an example. Table 2.1 presents different prices of Bubbly Pop and how many cans you might be willing and able to buy at each price.

According to Table 2.1, if the price of a single can of Bubbly Pop were 50 cents, you would be able and willing to buy 8 cans. If the price were $1.25, you would able and willing to buy 1 can. This is an example of a **demand schedule**. It shows, in table form, how many cans you would demand at a variety of prices. Notice that as the price increases from 50 cents to $1.50, you want fewer and fewer cans of Bubbly Pop. This is called the **law of demand**: As the price increases, the quantity demanded decreases. Figure 2.1 shows the exact same information in another form—a graph.

Notice that the law of demand is shown graphically as a line with a negative slope. As price goes down, quantity goes up. If you know a little math, you might be wondering at this point about the axes. Usually the independent variable is on the X-axis and the dependent variable is on the Y-axis. In

TABLE 2.1
Price and Quantity of Bubbly Pop

Price	Quantity
$0.50	8
$0.75	6
$1.00	3
$1.25	1
$1.50	0

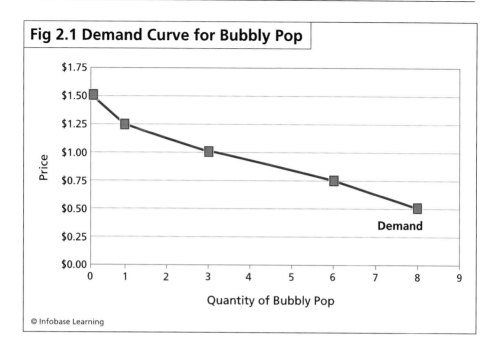

Fig 2.1 Demand Curve for Bubbly Pop

economics, we typically think of changes in price causing changes in quantity, meaning that price is the independent variable and quantity is the dependent variable. But in the graph above, price is where the dependent variable should be, and quantity is where the independent variable should be. An early economist, Alfred Marshall, presented the graph this way in one of the first economics textbooks to be published. This textbook was the best-selling economics book for over 60 years, so reversing the axes has just been an accepted practice ever since.

Now let's return to our Bubbly Pop example. Assume that on the day you are thinking about how much you are able and willing to pay for a can of Bubbly Pop, it is blistering hot outside. Would this affect your demand? As Table 2.2 shows, it probably would.

Because the temperature is so high, your willingness to pay has changed. At every price listed, you are willing to buy more. So at a price of 50 cents, you are now willing to buy 12 cans when before it got so hot you were only willing to buy 8. At a price of $1.50, you were not willing to buy any before, but because it is so hot, you are now willing to buy 3 cans.

Now let's consider another variable. Instead of the temperature being so hot, what if you suddenly had more income? Can you see how the new quantities might look similar to those below? In other words, if you have more income, you have more ability to buy, so you can demand more at every price. The old and new demand curves are shown in Figure 2.2.

TABLE 2.2
Bubbly Pop in a Heat Wave

Price and Quantity of Bubbly Pop		
Price	Original Quantity	New Quantity
$0.50	8	12
$0.75	6	10
$1.00	3	8
$1.25	1	5
$1.50	0	3

As you can see, the new curve in the graph (the green line) looks just like the curve in the old graph—it has a negative slope, indicating that as price falls, quantity demanded goes up. But it is displaced to the right of the first curve because of a change in the temperature or income. You can see on the graph exactly what we saw in the corresponding table. At a price of 50 cents, your demand was 8 cans, but this increased to 12 cans when it was very hot or if you had more income.

So far we have looked at two things that would change your demand for Bubbly Pop: temperature and income. In the real-world, there are a great number of things that might affect your demand for Bubbly Pop. Let's look at several of these one by one.

INCOME

We have already shown how income can change your demand for something, but we have discussed only one-half of the possibilities. In our example with Bubbly Pop, more income might mean that you would want more Bubbly Pop. If this were true, we would call Bubbly Pop a **normal good**. More generally, a normal good is simply something that you want more of, if you have more income. Besides Bubbly Pop, you can probably think of a lot of things that you would want more of if you had more money: CD's, vacations, steaks, etc. But there are some things that you would probably want less of if you had more money. For example, if you had more income, you would probably want less hamburger (you would want more expensive cuts of meat instead). Or, you might want fewer store-brand canned vegetables (you would want brand names or fresh). You might want less condensed soup or fewer "value meals" at

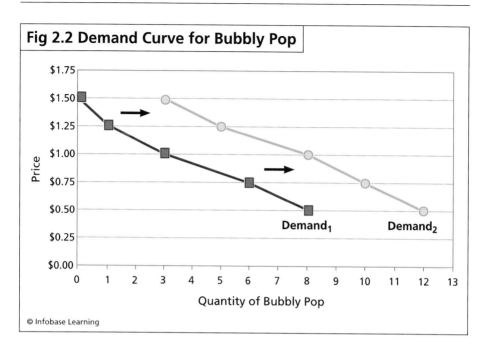

fast-food restaurants. We call those things that we want less of if our income increases **inferior goods**. Of course, both normal and inferior goods work in the opposite directions, too. So a normal good is one that you want more of when you have more money, but it is also one that you want less of if you have less money. In other words, your income and your demand for the good both move in the same direction (they both go up, or they both go down). An inferior good is one that you want less of if you have more money, but it is also one that you want more of if you have less money. Thus your income and your demand for an inferior good move in opposite directions (one goes up and the other goes down). Table 2.3 illustrates these patterns.

TABLE 2.3
Normal Goods and Inferior Goods

Normal Goods	Inferior Goods
Income ↑ ⟹ Demand ↑	Income ↑ ⟹ Demand ↓
Income ↓ ⟹ Demand ↓	Income ↓ ⟹ Demand ↑

Tastes and Preferences

A wide variety of things can affect tastes and preferences and, in turn, affect demand. The day being very hot (discussed above) is one example. Another example might be a drop in preference (and demand) for a product because of something bad coming to light about that product. The demand for peanut butter fell a few years ago when some jars were found to have been contaminated by harmful bacteria. The increase in demand for cell phones has been prompted by our society's increased reliance on them. And the demand for salt and salty foods has declined at least in part because the government has released several statements recently about the detrimental health effects of too much salt in our diets.

The Price of Substitutes or Complements

How much consumers are able and willing to buy of something depends upon not only the price of the good in question but also the price of other goods that they may want to buy. Returning to our Bubbly Pop example, what might happen to the quantity you demand at every price if you found out that the price of another cola drink, Zippy Pop, just decreased? Table 2.4 shows how this might affect your demand for Bubbly Pop.

As the table shows, if the price of Zippy Pop goes down, you want fewer cans of Bubbly Pop at each price. Why is that? If we consider Zippy Pop and Bubbly Pop to be **substitutes** (i.e., you could consume one or the other) and if the price of Zippy Pop falls, you are likely to switch your consumption away from Bubbly Pop to Zippy Pop because it is relatively cheaper. The graph representing this is

TABLE 2.4
Price and Substitutes

Price and Quantity of Bubbly Pop		
Price	Original Quantity	New Quantity
$0.50	8	6
$0.75	6	4
$1.00	3	1
$1.25	1	0
$1.50	0	0

shown in Figure 2.3. Conversely, if the price of Zippy Pop increased, you would probably want more Bubbly Pop (at every price) because now it would be relatively cheaper than Zippy Pop.

Sometimes goods are related to each other because they are substitutes. Other times, goods are related to each other because you use them together. What if a fast-food restaurant advertised that they were selling their hamburgers for half price? How would this affect your demand for Bubbly Pop? It would probably increase your demand because hamburgers and Bubbly Pop are consumed together—they are **complements.** Other examples are contact lenses and contact lens solution, DVDs and DVD players, peanut butter and jelly. All of these pairs of goods are used together. So if the price of one of them goes down, the demand for the other one goes up, even though the price of the latter has stayed exactly the same as it was. You would want more Bubbly Pop if you could get a hamburger for 50 percent less than before even though the price of Bubbly Pop did not change—it was the price of its complement that changed.

Expectations
Up until this point we have examined what happens to your demand for Bubbly Pop when various things actually do change: the product's own price, your

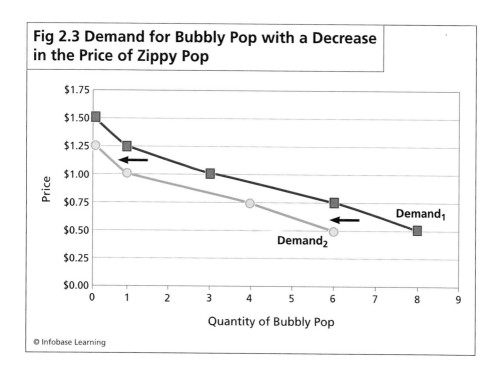

Fig 2.3 Demand for Bubbly Pop with a Decrease in the Price of Zippy Pop

© Infobase Learning

income, the temperature, the price of a competing brand, or the price of a hamburger. But sometimes our demand for something changes even when nothing actually happens. Sometimes all it takes is thinking that something *might* happen. Let's assume, for example, that you think the price of Bubbly Pop will increase next week. What would this belief or expectation do to your demand for Bubbly Pop right now? It would probably increase, right? You will most likely want to buy before the price goes up.

Expectations play an interesting role in consumer demand because they can become a self-fulfilling prophesy. If you expect the price to increase in the future, you will buy more today. But buying more today increases demand today, which in turn increases the price! Therefore, acting on expectations can bring about the very result you are expecting. Expectation in fact can strongly influence a broader range of economic behavior than deciding on how many cans of Bubbly Pop to buy today. Think of how this concept might apply to the stock market, which is affected by quite a number of significant expectations components. As traders act on their expectations about the future value of a stock, they often bring about the outcome they were expecting in the first place.

Population
The larger the population, the more demand there will be for goods and services. Sometimes, subgroups of a population cause increases in demand for

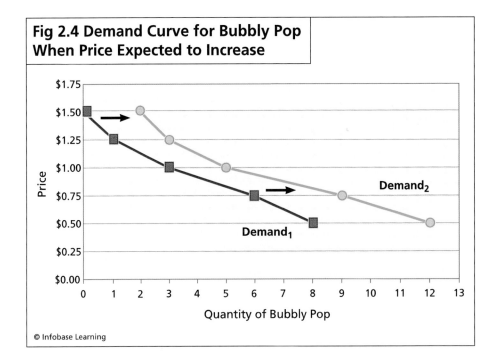

Fig 2.4 Demand Curve for Bubbly Pop When Price Expected to Increase

Price

Quantity of Bubbly Pop

Demand₂

Demand₁

© Infobase Learning

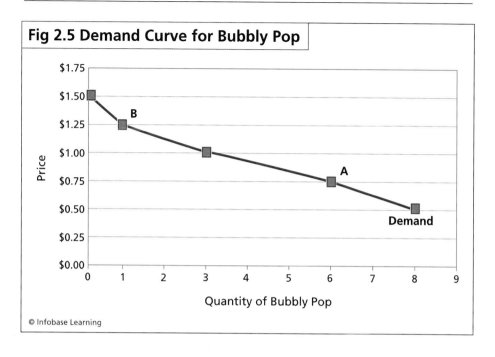

Fig 2.5 Demand Curve for Bubbly Pop

Price (y-axis): $0.00 to $1.75

Quantity of Bubbly Pop (x-axis): 0 to 9

B
A
Demand

© Infobase Learning

items geared toward a particular demographic. For example, as the Baby Boom generation grows older, demand for assisted living facilities, hair coloring, adult diapers—all the goods and services associated with aging—will increase.

CHANGES IN DEMAND AND CHANGES IN QUANTITY DEMANDED

In the first half of this chapter we examined several things that might cause consumers to change their demand for something. Per the law of demand, for example, the quantity that consumers demand changes when prices change. But we also know that other variables (ranging from changes in temperature to bacterial contaminants) also influence and change demand. At this point, we need to be more precise about the difference between changes in price and changes in other variables. To illustrate this distinction, we can go back to our original demand curve for Bubbly Pop.

When the price of Bubbly Pop increases from $0.75 to $1.25 a can, the number of cans of Bubbly Pop you want falls from 6 to 1. In other words, when the price of Bubbly Pop goes up, we move from point A to point B on the graph. Remember that changing the price of Bubbly Pop is how we got that graph in the first place—we changed the price, recorded the quantities, and then connected the dots. When the price of a good or service changes, the quantity demanded of that good or service also changes—it moves along a given demand curve and is called a **change in quantity demanded**. When we change the price, however, we continue to hold everything else (like income, prices of other goods, population, etc.) constant. If one of these other variables changes, the whole demand curve shifts, as we have seen in the previous graphs. We call that shift (as opposed to a movement along a curve) a **change in demand**.

The terminology may be a little confusing, but it is important to understand this distinction because this is what allows us to fully understand exactly what it is consumers are reacting to. For example, immediately after the 9/11 attacks, the price of gasoline went up. At the same time, consumers increased their consumption of gas. At first blush, this appears to be a violation of the law of demand—if the price of something increases, demand is supposed to fall, not increase. But a closer look tells a different story. What was happening was not a movement along one demand curve (where if price increases, quantity demanded decreases). Instead, the demand curve was shifting to the right, reflecting consumers' expectations that the price of gas would continue to rise in the future so it made sense to buy more gasoline before this occurred. Table 2.5 summarizes the difference.

SUPPLY

Now let's examine all of these concepts from the perspective of the other side of the market. To keep things simple, we'll use the same examples that were used to illustrate demand. A good place to begin is with the used car that was bought and sold over a kitchen table.

When you are buying a used car, the other side of the market is the person selling the car. In more general terms, the supply side of the market consists of companies providing products to the market. It is important to point out here that we are not talking about retail stores that sell products. Now let's

TABLE 2.5
Change in Quantity Demand vs. Change in Demand

Change in Quantity Demanded	Change in Demand
Caused by change in: • Price of specific good or service	Caused by change in: • Consumer Income • Tastes and Preferences • Prices of Other Goods • Expectations • Population
Looks Like: • Movement from one point to another on one demand curve	Looks Like: • Shift of entire demand curve, to the right (increase) or left (decrease)

TABLE 2.6
Price and Quantity of Bubbly Pop

Price	Quantity Demanded	Quantity Supplied
$0.50	8	3
$0.75	6	6
$1.00	3	8
$1.25	1	10
$1.50	0	11

go back to our Bubbly Pop example. Here the supply side of the market is not the convenience store that sells the Bubbly Pop. Instead, the supply side of the market is the manufacturer of Bubbly Pop.

Because the supply side of the market bears several similarities to the demand side (just a difference of perspective), we will not spend as much time developing the foundation. Going back to our Bubbly Pop example, pretend that you are the manufacturer of Bubbly Pop instead of the consumer. Just like the consumer, however, you need to decide how much you are willing to participate in the market when the price of Bubbly Pop fluctuates. The demand schedule we used above is reproduced here, with the addition of another column—quantity supplied.

Remember that the law of demand says that as price increases, quantity demanded will decrease. You can see this principle at work in the first two columns of our table. But when you look at the first and third columns, you see an entirely different relationship: As price increases, so does the quantity supplied. This is called the **law of supply**. When the market price is very low ($0.50), suppliers are willing to provide only 3 cans of Bubbly Pop to the market. Why? Because the price covers their costs of producing only 3 cans. When the price rises to $0.75, suppliers are willing to provide 6 cans to the market; when it rises to $1.00, they will provide 8 cans. The higher the price, the more units of a product suppliers are willing to provide because the higher price covers more of their costs of doing business. Suppliers would be very anxious to be active in the market if the market price rose to $1.50—they would provide 11 cans.

If we were to graph columns 1 and 3, we would get something like Figure 2.6. Notice that the slope of this supply curve is positive, showing exactly what we saw in the corresponding table: As price increases, firms are willing to provide more units of product to the market.

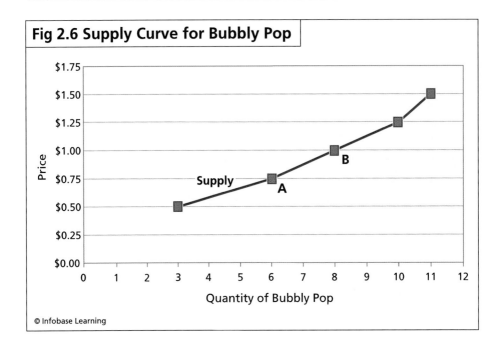

Fig 2.6 Supply Curve for Bubbly Pop

© Infobase Learning

Here the result is similar to what happens to the demand curve. When the market price changes, it causes a **change in quantity supplied**. In other words, we move from point A to point B on one supply curve. But again, as with demand, changes in other variables can also affect supply. And as with demand, when any of these things change, the whole supply curve shifts, causing a **change in supply**.

Prices of Inputs

Firms use a lot of different kinds of resources to produce their products. When the price of any of these inputs increases, it means that suppliers must get a higher market price to justify bringing their products to market. Let's assume for example that the price of sugar goes up. In light of this increase to their costs of doing business, the producers of Bubbly Pop will have to reevaluate how much they are willing to provide to the market. Table 2.7 illustrates what is likely to happen.

Notice that when the price of an input (sugar in this case) increases, suppliers are willing to supply only 5 cans at a market price of $1.25, whereas they were willing to provide 10 cans at the same market price when the price of sugar was lower. Again, this is because a price of $1.25 covers less of their production costs, which are now higher than before. Figure 2.7 shows the graph reflecting the new situation.

The other thing to notice about this graph is that this represents a **decrease in supply**. The supply curve shifts to the left, but looked at differently, it also looks

TABLE 2.7
How Input Affects Supply

Price	Quantity Demand	Old Quantity Supplied	New Quantity Supplied
$0.50	8	3	1
$0.75	6	6	2
$1.00	3	8	3
$1.25	1	10	5
$1.50	0	11	7

like it shifts slightly upward—not what you would expect if supply decreases. To avoid confusion, this discussion will refer to the supply curve shifting left (a decrease in supply) and shifting right (an increase in supply), not up or down. Thus, if input prices decrease, the supply curve would shift to the right, indicating that suppliers are willing to supply more at every price because their costs of production have fallen.

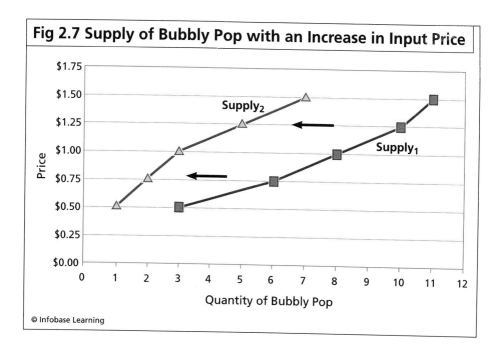

Fig 2.7 Supply of Bubbly Pop with an Increase in Input Price

Technology

Technological changes are closely related to changes in input prices. If advances in technology result in producers being able to produce more with the same inputs, then the supply curve will shift to the right (there will be an increase in supply).

Prices of Substitute Goods

Earlier in the chapter we showed how the prices of other goods can lead to changes in the demand for a product. Likewise, the prices of other goods can also lead to changes in the supply of a product. Firms can often switch from producing one good to another fairly easily if the resources used for both are similar. So if the price of another good that the firm can produce changes, it will change how much of the original good is supplied. For example, what if the firm that produces Bubbly Pop also makes Lemony Pop? Now assume there is an Internet rumor that drinking Lemony Pop lowers cholesterol, something that is likely to increase consumer interest in and demand for Lemony Pop. What do you expect the firm to do? If you said increase the supply of Lemony Pop, you are correct. But to do this, the firm must decrease the supply of Bubbly Pop. The firm still has the same resources, and these resources cannot accommodate producing the same quantity of Bubbly Pop if they are also to be used for increased production of Lemony Pop. Production of one product means reducing production of the other. Therefore, the supply curve for Bubbly Pop will shift to the left, representing a decrease in supply.

Expectations

Expectations also play a part in the supply side of the market. If Bubbly Pop manufacturers expect the price of Bubbly Pop to increase next month, what will they do today? They will stop providing Bubbly Pop to the market today, stockpile it, and then provide it to the market when the price increases next month when they can get a higher price for it. Just as with demand, however, this creates a self-fulfilling prophesy. Withholding the product from the market today does indeed drive up the price, (we'll see how this happens later), creating the higher price that the firm expected. We do not know if price really would have gone up next month or not, but if suppliers think that it will and adjust their output today accordingly, they will cause the price to go up. This happens quite frequently in the case of gasoline. As noted above, consumer expectations (and the corresponding increase in demand)can raise the price of gasoline. Suppliers also react to expectations about future gas prices, withholding gas from the market when they believe price will be higher in the near future.

Number of Firms

This variable is very simple: The more firms there are in the market producing something, the more of it there is. So when more firms producing flat screen

TVs entered the market, the supply of flat screen TVs increased, causing the supply curve to shift to the right.

EQUILIBRIUM

We have already explained equilibrium as a sort of "agreement" that occurs when the buyers and sellers in a market agree on a price. What transpires between a single buyer and single seller (e.g., when reaching an agreement on the price of a used car) also transpires between consumers that are buyers and businesses that are sellers. The communication is more complex, but as we discussed, the market has its own language in terms of goods piling up and not selling, versus goods flying off the shelves as consumers rush to buy them. Our final step in this initial discussion of demand and supply is to bring both sides of the market together. Let's revisit our example for Bubbly Pop (Table 2.6), which is reproduced here as Table 2.8 for easy reference.

Look more closely at the demand and supply quantities at each price. For example, if the market price for Bubbly Pop is $0.50, consumers are very happy. They want to buy 8 cans. Producers, on the other hand, are not very thrilled with this price. Fifty cents will not cover the costs of producing very many cans of Bubbly Pop. In fact, the producers are willing to provide only 3 cans to the market at this price. Now we have a problem. Consumers want 8 cans, but producers want to offer only 3 cans. Moreover, market exchanges are voluntary—neither side of the market is forced to participate. Therefore, producers cannot be compelled to provide more Bubbly Pop if doing so is unprofitable for them. So what happens if consumers want more Bubbly Pop than is available in the market place? Simple. They will start competing for the Bubbly Pop and bid the price up.

TABLE 2.8

Price and Quantity of Bubbly Pop

Price	Quantity Demanded	Quantity Supplied
$0.50	8	3
$0.75	6	6
$1.00	3	8
$1.25	1	10
$1.50	0	11

What if the market price were $1.25? As you might expect, producers are pleased with this, and they are willing to provide 10 cans to the market. Consumers do not like this price very much and are willing to buy only 1 can. Again, exchanges are voluntary, so consumers cannot be forced to buy more than 1 can of Bubbly Pop at this price. So those 9 extra cans will just sit on the shelf, collecting dust. This is a very clear signal to the producer: The price is too high!

Look at the table again. At what price do buyers and sellers come to agreement? In other words, at what price do producers sell all they have and consumers buy all they want? If you said $0.75, you are correct. At $0.75 consumers would like to buy 6 cans. At $0.75 producers will offer 6 cans for sale. There are no cans collecting dust on the shelf; there are no bidding wars on scarce cans. The price of $0.75 is the equilibrium price.

The graph in Figure 2.8 duplicates the same information we saw in the table above. At a price of $0.50, quantity demanded is more than quantity supplied. As a result, the market price increases. At a price of $1.50, just the reverse happens; there are more cans than people want, so the market price decreases. The equilibrium price, where quantity demanded equals quantity supplied, is $0.75. It is also where the demand and supply curves intersect. You might remember from your math classes that when two lines intersect, they are equal at that point—the very essence of equilibrium.

Now let's go back and examine some of the factors that can influence changes in demand (e.g., increased income, tastes and preferences, complements and

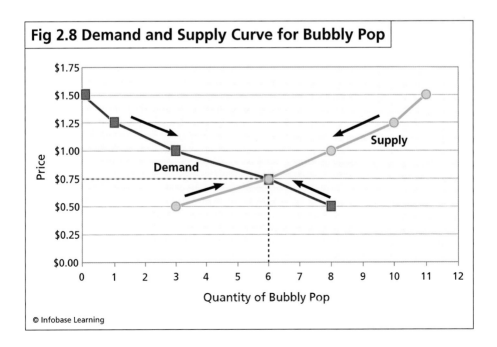

Fig 2.8 Demand and Supply Curve for Bubbly Pop

© Infobase Learning

Fig 2.9 Market for Bubbly Pop When Demand Increases

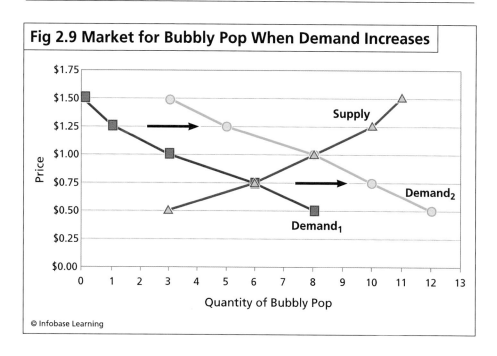

© Infobase Learning

substitutes, and expectations). For example, we discussed what would happen if consumers' incomes increased and the good is a normal good (meaning it's something people are likely to want more of). The demand curve would shift to the right, indicating that demand increases. So what happens to the market price and quantity when that happens?

As we can see in Figure 2.9, when income increases (and the good is a normal good), the demand for the good increases, shifting the demand curve to the right. This results in both a higher market price and a higher quantity exchanged. This occurs because at the old equilibrium price of $0.75, an increase in income causes consumers to now want 10 cans of Bubbly Pop instead of the 6 cans they previously wanted. But if the price is $0.75, producers are willing to provide only 6 cans to the market. Therefore, the increase in income causes an increase in demand. At the old equilibrium price of $0.75, there is more demand than supply, driving the price up to the new equilibrium price of $1.00.

What happens to the market price and quantity if supply changes? Here we can refer back to our discussion on changing input prices. Assume the price of sugar goes up. We already know that when the price of any input increases, the firm's costs of doing business also increase. This increase, in turn, means that the firm will be willing to supply a lower quantity at every price; that is, supply decreases. Remember that a decrease in supply is a shift of the curve to the left, resulting in something that looks like the graph

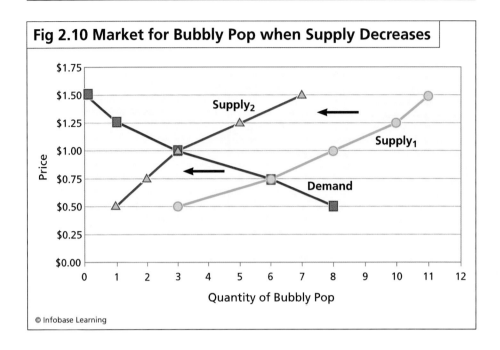

Fig 2.10 Market for Bubbly Pop when Supply Decreases

© Infobase Learning

presented in Figure 2.10. As the graph shows, when supply decreases, the market price gets pushed up (from $0.75 to $1.00), and the quantity exchanged on the market falls (from 6 to 3).

BROWN EGGS OR WHITE?

Now we have all the tools we need to answer the first question posed in the introduction to this chapter: Why do brown eggs cost more than white eggs? Many people think that there is a nutritional difference between brown eggs and white eggs, but there is not. Brown eggs are not better for you; brown eggs are not organic. In fact, there is no difference between brown and white eggs except the color of the shell. So why are brown eggs more expensive? You might think that even though they are nutritionally equivalent, people *think* that they are better, making the demand for brown eggs greater and thus explaining the higher price. Almost . . . but not quite. Let's take a look at how that answer would look graphically.

If people (mistakenly) think that brown eggs are better for you and this results in a greater demand for them, the demand curve for brown eggs will lie to the right of that of white eggs, as in the graph shown in Figure 2.11. This would cause the price of brown eggs to be higher than that of white eggs ($P_B > P_W$). No problem there. But look what else is going on in this market—the quantity of brown eggs would also be higher than the quantity of white eggs ($Q_B > Q_W$). But that is not the case. Walk into almost any grocery store and

Fig 2.11 The Market for White and Brown Eggs

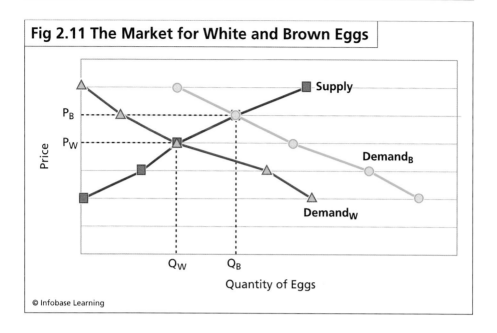

you will see many more white eggs for sale than brown eggs. So a difference in demand cannot be the answer.

Eliminating demand side explanations, we are left with the supply side. There must be some difference in the supply of brown eggs and white eggs that cause the price of brown eggs to be higher and the quantity of brown eggs to be lower as compared to white eggs. Now look at how this is represented in Figure 2.12.

In this graph, the supply of brown eggs lies to the left of that of white eggs. This graph explains what we observe: Brown eggs are higher in price ($P_B > P_W$) but there are fewer of them than there are white eggs ($Q_W > Q_B$). So, brown eggs cost more than white eggs because the supply of brown eggs is less than that of white eggs. But why? Remember that one reason the supply curve shifts to the left is that it represents an increase in the costs of doing business. Therefore, brown eggs must be costlier to produce than white eggs, and in fact, they are. Brown eggs are laid by Rhode Island Red chickens, which are bigger (requiring more feed) than the chickens that lay white eggs.

PRICE FLOORS AND CEILINGS

As previously noted, the market automatically adjusts when prices are too high (above the equilibrium price) or too low (below the equilibrium price). When the price of a good or service is anything other than at equilibrium, the situation results in a "dialog" between buyers and sellers, and the price is adjusted accordingly. But what if this doesn't happen?

Fig 2.12 The Market for White and Brown Eggs

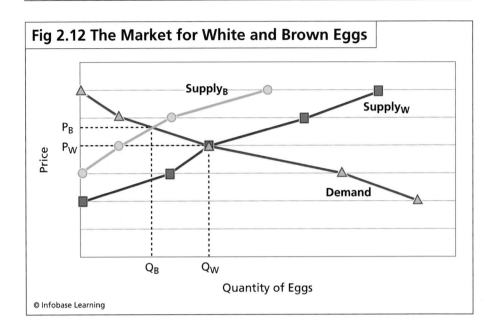

Price

Supply_B

Supply_W

P_B

P_W

Demand

Q_B   Q_W

Quantity of Eggs

© Infobase Learning

Let's look again at our market for Bubbly Pop, only this time we'll assume that the market price is not the equilibrium price of $0.75. Instead, the price is $0.50. First we need to determine why the price is "stuck" at $0.50, when it is clear that market forces should push the price up to $0.75. One reason is that the government sometimes steps into markets and sets limits on prices. In this case, if the government believed that the market clearing, or equilibrium price, of $0.75 was too high, it might simply mandate that in this market for Bubbly Pop, the price may not rise above $0.50. In other words, the government puts a cap, or a **ceiling**, on how high the price can rise.

Why would the government do this? The government gets involved in some markets by setting a price ceiling because it believes that the interests of consumers are best served by keeping the price low. Figure 2.13 shows the result of a price ceiling in this market.

If the government sets a price ceiling of $0.50 on Bubbly Pop, consumers will, in fact, pay a lower price than they would pay if the market had set the price. Sounds good, right? You can now buy Bubbly Pop for 25 cents less than you would be paying if the market had determined the price. At a price of $0.50, you and other consumers will now demand 8 cans, not the 6 cans you would buy if the market price were $0.75. But remember that exchanges in the market are voluntary. Although the government can set a price ceiling at $0.50, it cannot compel suppliers to produce 8 cans. In fact, producers will respond to the mandated price of $0.50 by reducing production to 3 cans. When we analyzed this situation earlier, we pointed out that market forces drove the price up to

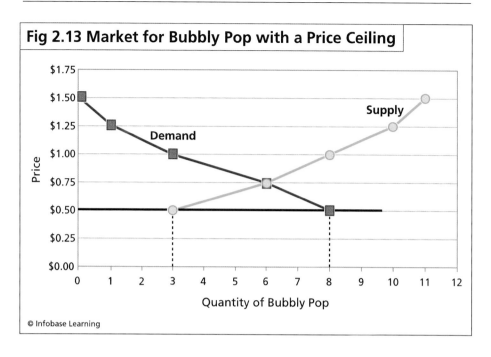

Fig 2.13 Market for Bubbly Pop with a Price Ceiling

$0.75, the equilibrium price. But now there is an obstacle to market force adjust-ments—the government has forbidden any price increase. The result is that con-sumers want 8 cans, producers will produce only 3 cans, and this means there will be a shortage of 5 cans. So, although some consumers will benefit from the lower price (the ones able to buy the 3 cans), not all consumers will benefit. Because of the shortage, some won't be able to buy any Bubbly Pop at all. In general, price ceilings benefit consumers who can find and purchase a good or service (because the price is lower than it otherwise would have been), but not all consumers who want the good or service can get it.

Whenever there is a shortage of something, some way must be found to allocate the units that do exist. In an unrestricted market, price does this—whoever is able and willing to buy will find enough of the product to purchase because the product will be exchanged for the equilibrium price. When the market is restricted, as in the case of a price ceiling, there are not enough units available to go around and some other way must be found to decide who will get the product and who will not. Some allocation methods include a first-come first-served approach or a lottery system. In any case, some unmet demand in the market remains.

It should be noted that the government does not generally put price ceilings on goods like soda pop. One real-world example, however, can be found in New York City where the municipal government puts a price ceiling on the amount of rent that can be charged for some apartments (resulting in long waiting lists for apartments). Another example comes from the late 1970s when the United States was faced with two oil embargos that threatened to drive gas prices very high, and the government imposed a price ceiling on gasoline (resulting in long lines at the pumps).

But what would happen if the government (instead of being concerned about keeping consumer prices low) decided that the interests of the producers of Bubbly Pop would be best served if the price were higher than $0.75? In this case, the government could set a **price floor** at $1.25, meaning that the price of Bubbly Pop was not to fall below that price. The graph for this situation would look like Figure 2.14.

Now we have a different problem. As the graph shows, producers are quite willing to supply 10 cans to the market at this higher price, but at $1.25 per can, consumers want to buy only 1 can. The result is a surplus of Bubbly Pop—9 cans, to be exact. What do we do with this excess?

In the real world, price floors (or **price supports**, as they are sometimes called) are not applied to products like Bubbly Pop. They are most often utilized in agricultural markets. When this results in a surplus of some crop, the government will often buy up this surplus and store it, or send it overseas as part of one or more U.S. international relief programs. This, in effect, brings an additional player into the market. Now, we have buyers, sellers, and the government, which will buy whatever quantity producers supply in excess of what consumers demand.

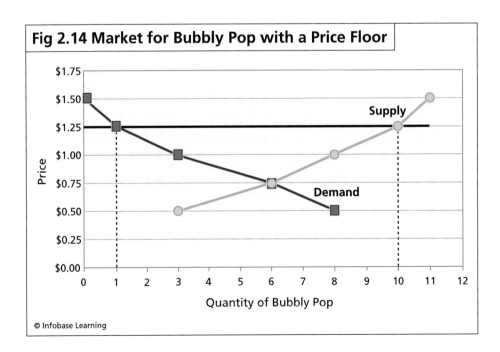

Fig 2.14 Market for Bubbly Pop with a Price Floor

Price / Quantity of Bubbly Pop

Supply

Demand

© Infobase Learning

Now we are ready to answer the second question posed at the beginning of this chapter: Why is there a shortage of transplant organs? Your first response was probably something like, "Because there is more demand for organs than existing supply." That is certainly true because demand for available organs does indeed exceed supply. But how do you reconcile this with the theories you have already learned about demand and supply—specifically, that if demand for something exceeds supply, price ordinarily adjusts upward until the shortage disappears? Somehow, this theory does not apply to the market for transplantable organs because shortages persist. So we are still left with the question of why demand for organs so consistently exceeds supply. As we discussed above, the only way for a shortage to persist is if there is something blocking the upward movement of price. In other words, a price ceiling exists in the market for organs. In fact, the government has made it illegal to sell organs for transplant, effectively setting the price of organs at $0. The shortage of transplantable organs will disappear if one (or more) of the following occurs:

The supply of organs increases. This is a shift of the supply curve to the right, resulting in a larger quantity of transplantable organs. Two ways to accomplish this are getting people to designate themselves as organ donors on their driver's licenses and increasing development of artificial organs.

The demand for organs decreases. Preventive health measures to make organ transplants unnecessary would reduce the demand for organs.

Raise the price of organs. The government, by declaring the sale of organs illegal, has effectively set a price of $0. If you try to sell an organ for more than the price of $0, you may be arrested—that's a pretty effective way of maintaining a price ceiling! To eliminate the shortage, the government could remove the prohibition against selling organs, and let the market decide on organ prices. But whereas this is a market solution, many doctors, medical ethicists, and others are uncomfortable with this solution. This dilemma is a good example of something discussed earlier in this chapter—specifically, the idea that the market has no conscience. With respect to transplant organs, a market solution may not be a solution that we, as a society, feel comfortable with.

SUMMARY

Although all of economics cannot be reduced to the relationship between supply and demand, this relationship is very important in explaining a large part of the economic structure and activity of the world we live in. The information presented in this chapter shows that what occurs between an individual buyer and seller, extends to what occurs at the market level: In either case, the laws of demand and supply determine agreement on equilibrium price, and the same sort of communication occurs at both levels (individual and market). Communication between many buyers and sellers establishes a market-clearing price and quantity. When changes in buyers' and/or sellers' circumstances occur, the demand and/or supply curves shift, establishing new prices and quantities.

If the government believes a market price to be too high or too low, it can establish a price ceiling or floor. Price ceilings result in shortages, whereas price floors result in surpluses. Because market price is no longer the allocation method, some other way must be devised to decide who will buy and sell the available units.

Understanding the basics of demand and supply can answer many questions that, at first look, may not appear to be economic questions. Later chapters in this book will build on this foundation to answer many more questions.

Further Reading

Bauman, Y. *A Cartoon Introduction to Microeconomics.* New York: Hill and Wang Publishers, 2010.

Harford, T. *The Undercover Economist.* New York: Random House, 2007.

Landsburg, S.E. *Armchair Economist: Economics and Everyday Life.* New York: The Free Press, 1993.

Levitt, S.J., and S.J. Dubner. *Freakonomics: A Rogue Economist Explains the Hidden Side of Everything.* New York: HarperCollins, 2005.

————. *Superfreakonomics: Global Cooling, Patriotic Prostitutes, and Why Suicide Bombers Should Buy Life Insurance.* New York: HarperCollins, 2009.

Wheelan, C. *The Naked Economics: Undressing the Dismal Science.* New York: W. W. Norton, 2009.

## CHAPTER 3

ELASTICITY

INTRODUCTION

As Chapter 2 illustrated, understanding the basics of demand and supply can answer some interesting questions. In fact, the law of demand and the law of supply are important components of knowing how the world works. You know, for example, that if a commodity's price increases, consumers will want fewer units, but producers will want to produce more units. But how much more? Based on the laws of demand and supply we can reasonably know the direction of the quantity change when the price changes, but we cannot predict the magnitude of the quantity change. In other words, Chapter 2 focused on determining *how* quantity changes when price changes; the focus of this chapter is *how much.*

You might wonder why going this extra step is important. Isn't knowing the "how" enough? What can you possibly gain from knowing "how much"? Plenty—and not just in theory! Knowing the "how much" is something that can explain any number of things that apply to your own life as well as the economics of the world you live in. You may have wondered, for example, why last-minute airline tickets are so expensive whereas last-minute Broadway show tickets are so cheap. Or imagine that you play an instrument in your city's symphony, and there is a disagreement over what the concert ticket prices should be. Some argue that the price should be low so more people will come. Others argue that the price should be higher—fewer people would come but the symphony would make more on each ticket sold. If the goal of the symphony is to make as much money as possible, both arguments sound plausible, but obviously, both cannot be correct. These are the kinds of questions addressed in this chapter. And, as you may have guessed, all of the answers are related to "how much?"

BASICS OF ELASTICITY

When we address the question of how much quantity changes when price does, what we are talking about is **elasticity**. Elasticity simply means responsiveness, so the real question becomes "How responsive is quantity to price changes?" For example, when the price of something goes up, we know that consumers will demand fewer units of that something. But do they want a lot less, or just a little less? In other words, how responsive are they to the price increase? Alternatively, if price falls, consumers will demand more—a lot more, or just a little more? As you will soon see, knowing how responsive consumers are to price changes is an important piece of information to have. (Note: Suppliers also have different degrees of responsiveness, but this chapter will focus on the demand side of things.)

MEASURING ELASTICITY OF DEMAND

One of the nice things about the concept of elasticity is that we do not have to be content with using vague terms, such as "consumers are very responsive" or "consumers are not very responsive" to price changes. Instead, we can measure elasticity of demand fairly precisely. We will not concern ourselves here with how this formula economists use to measure elasticity is derived; we will simply explain how to use it and what information it tells us:

Own Price Elasticity of Demand:

$$E = \frac{\text{Percentage change in Q}}{\text{Percentage change in P}}$$

Formula for Computing Elasticity of Demand:

$$E = \frac{Q_2 - Q_1}{P_2 - P_1} \times \frac{P_2 + P_1}{Q_2 + Q_1}$$

The top equation is the general formula for own price elasticity of demand, expressed as percentage changes. This calculation is called "own" price elasticity of demand because it measures how much consumers change their quantity demanded for a good when that good's price changes. The bottom equation is the one we will use to compute percentage changes. Later in the chapter, we will explain how quantity changes when another factor (other than own price) changes. Let's work through an example to see what these formulas tell us.

The best place to begin is to revisit the question about the price of symphony tickets. Assume that tickets have usually been priced at $5 each and that the typical turn-out for a symphony production has been 300 people. Further assume that the board of directors has been swayed by the lower price argument, so ticket prices have been lowered to $4 each. The board knows that more people will come at the lower price, and sure enough, attendance goes up to 350 people. Was this the right thing to do?

To answer this question we first need to determine the elasticity of demand for symphony tickets. Notice that the formula has two price/quantity pairs: P_1 and Q_1, and P_2 and Q_2. The "1s" designate the original price and quantity; the "2s" indicate the new price and quantity. In this instance, the original price per ticket was $5, so that is P_1. When the price was $5, the quantity was 300, so 300 is Q_1. The price was changed to $4—that's P_2. And when the price was lowered, quantity changed to 350—Q_2.

$$P_1 = \$5$$
$$Q_1 = 300$$

$$P_2 = \$4$$
$$Q_2 = 350$$

$$E = \frac{350 - 300}{4 - 5} \times \frac{4 + 5}{350 + 300} = \frac{50}{-1} \times \frac{9}{650} = \frac{450}{-650} = -0.69$$

After we plug in these numbers and do the calculation, our result is that the elasticity of demand for symphony tickets is −0.69. What does this number tell us? The first thing you should notice is that the number is negative. Take a minute to see if you can figure out why. First look at the numbers we plugged into the formula. The right-hand side of the formula involves adding numbers, so we do not get the negative number from there. The left-hand side of the formula is the difference in the quantities (expressed as the numerator) and the difference in the prices (expressed as the denominator). But notice that as the quantity decreases in the numerator (from 350 to 300), the price in the denominator increases (from 4 to 5). In fact, it is the price decrease that causes the quantity increase. Remember from Chapter 2 that price and quantity have an inverse relationship. Mathematically speaking, this means that under normal circumstances, the elasticity of demand will always be a negative number. Because of this, we will be using the absolute value of the number (i.e., ignoring the minus sign) in discussing elasticity.

Now let's move on to the magnitude of the number and what that means. In our example, we came up with an elasticity of demand for concert tickets of –0.69. Going back to the general expression for elasticity, we plug 0.69 in for the result:

$$-0.69 = \frac{\text{Percentage change in Q}}{\text{Percentage change in P}}$$

Now we can address some "what ifs." What if we decreased ticket prices by 10 percent? What would happen to the number of tickets we sell? Let's see. By plugging 10 percent into the denominator, we get:

$$-0.69 = \frac{\text{Percentage change in Q}}{-10}$$

To answer our question, we just need to solve for the numerator:

$$-0.69 \times -10 = \text{Percentage change in Q, or}$$
$$+6.9 = \text{Percentage change in Q.}$$

So, if we decrease ticket prices by 10 percent, we know (from Chapter 2) that we will sell more tickets. Now we also know that we will sell 6.9 percent more tickets. So a price reduction of 10 percent results in a quantity increase of 6.9 percent—an amount that is less than the price change. This indicates that people do not seem to be very responsive to the price reduction. They do demand more tickets, but their demand does not increase very much. The term that defines this lukewarm (low demand) response to price changes is **inelastic**. Do not make the mistake of thinking that inelastic demand means no response. Consumers do respond, but their response is fairly weak. In this case, lowering ticket prices makes consumer demand for quantity of tickets rise, but not by much.

Can you predict what will happen if we raise ticket prices? If you answered consumers would demand less, but not much less, you are correct. If we increase prices by 10 percent, we will sell 6.9 percent fewer tickets—again, quantity changes by a smaller percentage than price does.

Let's tweak the numbers in our example a little. Assume that when we lower ticket prices to $4, we sell 400 tickets. Plugging in our new numbers, we get:

$$P_1 = \$5$$
$$Q_1 = 300$$
$$P_2 = \$4$$
$$Q_2 = 400$$

$$E = \frac{400 - 300}{4 - 5} \times \frac{4 + 5}{400 + 300} = \frac{100}{-1} \times \frac{9}{70} = \frac{900}{-700} = -1.29$$

Now our result is –1.29. In this case, if we lower ticket prices by 10 percent, the quantity sold will increase by 12.9 percent. Conversely, if we raise ticket prices by 10 percent, we will sell 12.9 percent fewer tickets. Clearly, consumers are much more responsive to this second scenario than to the first. This is an example of an **elastic** demand. These two cases of elasticity are summarized in Table 3.1.

You might be wondering what it means if the elasticity is exactly equal to 1 (instead of being greater or less than 1)? That situation is covered in the next section, where we add the final piece of information needed to interpret elasticity.

ELASTICITY AND TOTAL REVENUE

Let's go back to our example and question regarding symphony ticket prices. If the symphony wants to generate as much money as possible, should prices be lowered, to attract more people, or should they be raised, to make more money on each ticket sold? The preceding section gave us some clues about the answer. Using our original numbers (when price is $4, 350 tickets will be sold), we know that changing ticket prices by 10 percent (either higher or lower) results in a quantity change in the opposite direction, that is 6.9 percent (lower or higher). The elasticity of demand for tickets is inelastic, so people don't respond much when the price changes. Let's take this one more step and look at what happens to **total revenue** under the two elasticity conditions.

Total revenue is the total amount of money made when something is sold: price × quantity. If the price is $5 and we sell 2 tickets, total revenue is $10. Notice we are not taking costs into account. So, our question about the symphony tickets is really asking, what will increase our gross revenue: increasing ticket prices or decreasing them?

TABLE 3.1
Elastic and Inelastic Demand

Term	Meaning	Magnitude (absolute value)
Inelastic	Consumers do not respond very much to price changes	$E < 1$
Elastic	Consumers are very responsive to price changes	$E > 1$

We can answer this question intuitively. If price increases and quantity does not change, what will happen to total revenue (TR)? Because TR = P × Q, if price goes up and quantity stays the same, total revenue will also increase. But we know that quantity will change if price goes up—it will decrease. Let's assume that the elasticity of demand for tickets is inelastic (−0.69). Remember what this means—when price changes, quantity changes in the opposite direction, but just a little bit. So price goes up (increasing total revenue), but quantity goes down (decreasing total revenue). But because the demand is inelastic, the quantity decrease is small and is more than offset by the price increase. The net effect on total revenue is that it increases:

$$TR = P \times Q$$

If demand is inelastic, when price increases, quantity decreases—a little:

$$TR = {\uparrow}P \times {\downarrow}Q = {\uparrow}TR$$

The price increase pushes total revenue up, the quantity decrease pushes total revenue down, but the price increase is more than the quantity decrease, so the final result is that total revenue increases.

If price decreases, total revenue also decreases. As a result of the lower price, quantity increases, but because demand is inelastic, quantity increases only slightly. The net effect on total revenue is that it decreases.

$$TR = {\downarrow}P \times {\uparrow}Q = {\downarrow}TR$$

As you can see from the equations above, if demand is inelastic, price and total revenue move in the same direction whether price increases or decreases. What if demand is elastic? Remember that this means that when price changes, consumers are very responsive, so quantity changes (in the opposite direction) a lot.

$$TR = P \times Q$$

If demand is elastic, when price increases, quantity decreases—a lot:

$$TR = {\uparrow}P \times {\downarrow}Q = {\downarrow}TR$$

The price increase pushes total revenue up, the quantity decrease pushes total revenue down, but the price increase is less than the quantity decrease, so the final result is that total revenue decreases.

If price decreases, total revenue increases. As a result of the lower price, quantity increases, but because demand is elastic, quantity increases by a lot. The net effect on total revenue is that it increases.

$$TR = \downarrow P \times \uparrow Q = \uparrow TR$$

Once again, we can generalize our result: When demand is elastic, price and total revenue move in opposite directions, again whether price increases or decreases. Table 3.2 summarizes these results.

What happens if the elasticity of demand is equal to 1? If this is the case, then a 10 percent decrease in price would lead to a 10 percent increase in quantity. Can you anticipate what the effect on total revenue would be? Total revenue would remain unchanged because (in percentage terms) the price decrease and quantity increase would exactly offset each other.

With this information, we now have a complete answer to our question about symphony tickets. With our original example (when Q2 = 350), we computed an elasticity of demand for symphony tickets of −0.69. This means that demand is inelastic because the absolute value of the number is less than 1. We now know that if the demand for symphony tickets is inelastic, the way to increase total revenue is to increase price. This may seem counterintuitive. After all, if the price is raised, fewer people will attend. That is true, but the increase in the price per ticket will more than make up for the reduction in the number of people.

When we used our second scenario (Q2 = 400), we discovered that demand is elastic (E = −1.29). With an elastic demand, if we want to increase total revenue, the price should be lowered. Although less money is made on each ticket, the increase in the number of tickets will more than make up for the lower price for each one.

These examples provide a very easy way for anyone in business to determine what to do with price. To use price elasticity, you simply need two price/

TABLE 3.2
Elasticities and Total Revenue

	Inelastic	Elastic
When P Increases	Total Revenue Increases	Total Revenue Decreases
When P Decreases	Total Revenue Decreases	Total Revenue Increases

quantity pairs: When price is $X, how many are sold? When price is $Y, how many are sold? The answer comes from substituting these values into the formula to determine the actual elasticity. If the absolute value of that number is less than 1, you have to increase price to increase total revenue. If the value is greater than 1, you have to lower the price to increase total revenue. Because the appropriate changes in price are inverse (exactly opposite to each other), it is clear that knowing the price elasticity is a very important piece of information.

DETERMINANTS OF ELASTICITY

There are several things that determine what the elasticity of a good or service will be. Consumers will be more responsive to the price changes of some things, just because of the nature of the products. At other times, circumstances may determine how responsive consumers will be. This section gives a brief synopsis of the major determinants of price elasticity of demand.

Is It a Necessity?

If something is a necessity, consumers are likely to not respond very much to price changes. When the price of gasoline increases, for example, do you reduce your consumption by a little or a lot? What about prescription drugs—when the price goes up, do you buy a few pills less? Many pills less? How about electricity? You might think that with goods like these, your consumption would not fall at all if the price increases. After all, if you need something, you will pay anything, right? Not exactly. You might be willing to pay a lot, but not an excessive amount. Even with goods that people need, the demand relationship is negative, so if price increases, the quantity demand will decrease. But it will not decrease by very much—demand for goods that are necessities is very inelastic.

Let's look at some additional examples. When the price of gasoline goes up, people continue to buy it. But they also take measures that allow them to cut down how much they buy. They might start car pooling, or riding a bike, or walking. They might also try to run all their errands at one time, avoid jackrabbit starts at lights, and make sure to keep their cars tuned and running at peak efficiency. When the price of electricity increases, similar conservation efforts usually occur: Consumers turn down the thermostat (or turn it up, depending on the season); they are more aware of turning off lights when leaving rooms; they replace standard light bulbs with energy efficient bulbs. Even with something like prescription medication, people will find ways to cut back—they buy generic, they look to alternative medicines, and sometimes they skip doses. With all of these examples, it is important to recognize that the basic demand relationship still exists: When price changes, the quantity demand changes in the opposite direction. But the strength of that relationship is weak. Quantity changes, but not by very much.

Homeowners can combat high utility bills by conserving energy, like turning down the thermostat. However, they still need heat and power, so this demand is considered inelastic.

It is perhaps easier to see that necessities have an inelastic demand if we think of consumers' responses to prices that go down instead of up. We know from the demand relationship that when the price of a good or service decreases, consumers will want more of that good or service. In the case of necessities, that relationship still holds, but consumers will not want very much more. For example, if the price of gasoline falls, consumers will buy more, but how much more can you buy? You might take that long road trip vacation or leave your car idling when you could have turned it off, but you are not going to drastically increase your consumption. If the price of electricity falls, you may not engage in as many conservation activities. You may keep your home warmer in the winter and cooler in the summer, but you will not increase your demand by a lot.

Are There Substitutes?

This determinant of elasticity is related to the question of whether the good or service is a necessity. If there are no (or few) substitutes for something, consumers will not be very sensitive to price changes. Alternatively, if something has a lot of substitutes consumers' demand is likely to change a lot in response to price changes. Think of what would happen if the price of Pepsi™ increased a lot. We know that consumers would reduce their consumption of Pepsi™, but by how much? It is likely that demand would fall by quite a bit because there are numerous substitutes for the soft drink, so the demand would be elastic.

On the other hand, what if the price of a loaf of bread increased? Would demand fall by a little or a lot? Probably by just a little. There are some substitutes—bagels, English muffins, wraps—but even these are not close substitutes, so the demand for bread would be fairly inelastic.

How Broadly Is the Category Defined?

You may have noticed in the example above that one good was very specific (Pepsi™) while the other example was broad (bread). The more broadly we define a good or service, the more inelastic the demand for it is. Continuing with our two examples, while the demand for Pepsi™ is elastic, the demand for soda pop is inelastic. The demand for bread is inelastic, but the demand for Pepperidge Farm™ bread is elastic. Why? Because the more broadly we define the category, the fewer substitutes something has. As we discussed, there are not many close substitutes for bread, but there are many substitutes for Pepperidge Farm™ bread. Along the same lines, your demand for breakfast cereal will be more inelastic than your demand for Kellogg's Frosted Flakes™.

How Long Is the Time Period?

Recall that the demand for gasoline is inelastic because gasoline is a necessity, and there are no substitutes. If the price of gas goes up tomorrow, you can cut back a little, but not really all that much. But if you had more time to adjust to the price increase, you could trade in your car for a more fuel efficient one, you could move closer to your workplace or school, you could find a car pool. In other words, the longer the time period, the more opportunities you have to adjust your behavior and find a way to buy less gas. Therefore, the longer the time period, the more elastic the demand becomes for the same good.

How Big a Part of Your Budget Is It?

If something takes up a very large part of your budget, the demand for it will be relatively elastic. Conversely, if the price of a good or service increases and it takes up a very small part of your budget, you are not likely to be very sensitive to that price increase. For example, if the price of salt increases, will you drastically cut back on your consumption of salt? Probably not—how often do you buy salt, after all? But what about your cell phone service? If the price of your service increases, you will probably respond to a much greater extent (cut back on the number of calls or texts, or even transfer your service altogether), because it is a relatively large part of your budget.

Table 3.3 presents price elasticities of demand for various goods and services. We see that the determinants of elasticity discussed above are evident in these real-world elasticities. Notice that consumers are much more sensitive to the price change of all breakfast cereals than of one particular cereal. We also see that goods like gasoline, cigarettes, and toothpaste, which have few (if any) substitutes and/or are necessities, have very small elasticities of demand. By contrast, the elasticity of demand for DVDs from Amazon is very large (consumers are very sensitive to price changes) because there are many substitutes.

ELASTICITY AND THE DEMAND CURVE

One final note about own price elasticity. Since elasticity is about how one variable changes in response to changes in another variable, you may be thinking that it sounds a lot like the definition of the slope of a line: how Y changes when

TABLE 3.3
Price Elasticity for Various Goods and Services

Product	Estimated Elasticity
Post™ Raisin Bran	−2.5
All breakfast cereals	−0.9
Restaurant meals	−0.67
Cigarettes	−0.25
Coca-Cola	−1.22
Grapes	−1.18
Gasoline (short-run)	−0.26
Gasoline (long-run)	−0.58
Milk	−0.04
DVDs from Amazon	−3.10
Toothpaste	−0.45

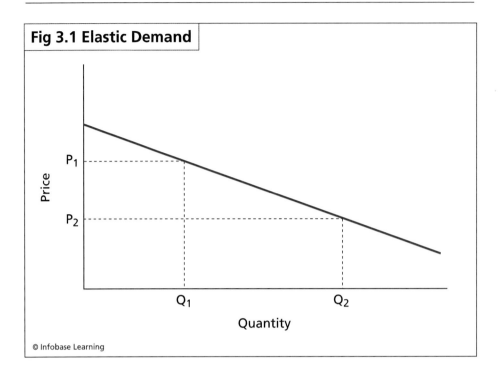

Fig 3.1 Elastic Demand

© Infobase Learning

X changes. Although elasticity is not the same thing as a slope, it is related. Remember that elasticity is not defined by how many units of a quantity change when price changes. It is defined by the percentage change in quantity caused by a percentage change in price.

Therefore, elasticity is not synonymous with slope, but it is related to slope. In general, the flatter a demand curve is, the more elastic it is. Conversely, the steeper the demand curve, the more inelastic it is. With both demand curves, we assume that price falls, from P_1 to P_2. As a result, quantity demand increases in each case, from Q_1 to Q_2. The size of the quantity change is very different, however. On the graph in Figure 3.1 (with an elastic demand curve), the quantity changes by a large amount, while the quantity change on the graph in Figure 3.2 is very small.

CROSS-PRICE ELASTICITY

The section above explained how we can measure and interpret the elasticity of a good or service. In other words, how sensitive consumers are to changes in the price of a good or service. But we know that there are factors other than price that determine the demand for a good or service. One of those other factors is the price of a related good. Remember from Chapter 2 that there are two categories of related goods: substitutes and complements. Because elasticity is just a measure of sensitivity, we can also measure how sensitive the demand for

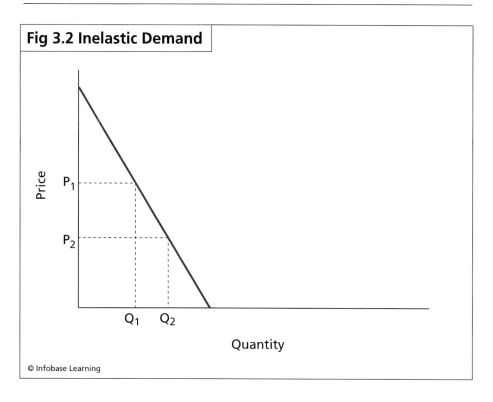

Fig 3.2 Inelastic Demand

© Infobase Learning

something is when the price of a related product changes. Let's begin by looking at the formula for cross-price elasticity of demand.

$$E_C = \frac{\text{Percentage change in } Q_x}{\text{Percentage change in } P_y}$$

Formula for Computing Cross Price Elasticity of Demand:

$$E_C = \frac{Q_{x2} - Q_{x1}}{P_{y2} - P_{y1}} \times \frac{P_{y2} + P_{y1}}{Q_{x2} + Q_{x1}}$$

The first thing you probably notice about this new formula is that it looks a lot more complicated than the own price elasticity formula. But look closer—it is really the same formula; the only difference is that we have now differentiated between the quantity of one product (X) and the price of another product (Y). In other words, **cross-price elasticity** answers the question: When the price of Y changes, how much do consumers change their consumption of X? For example, when the price of contact lenses increases, how many fewer bottles of contact lens solution do consumers buy? We know that lenses and solution are complements, so when the price of one increases, the demand for the other decreases. The cross-price elasticity measures the decrease in demand (how much). As another example, when the price of Coca-Cola™ increases, we know that consumers will buy more Pepsi™ because each is a substitute for the other. So the cross-price elasticity between the two tell how much more Pepsi™ consumers will buy as a result of the price increase of Coca-Cola.™

Let's look at a more detailed example of how cross-price elasticity works. Assume that a fast-food restaurant is running a special. A large order of fries is usually $1.99, but the special offer is a large order for $0.99. The restaurant owners know that they will sell more fries, because of the basic demand relationship. But they also notice that the fries special has changed something else: The quantity of soda pop they sell has now increased from 200 cups to 400 cups. Let's plug these amounts into the formula:

$$P_{Y1} = \$1.99$$
$$Q_{X1} = 200$$
$$P_{Y2} = \$0.99$$
$$Q_{X2} = 400$$

$$E_c = \frac{400 - 200}{.99 - 1.99} \times \frac{1.99 - .99}{200 + 400} = \frac{200}{-1} \times \frac{2.98}{600} = \frac{596}{-600} = -0.99$$

Before we examine this result, let's look at another example. Assume that the same fast-food restaurant runs another special, this time lowering the price of chicken sandwiches from $3.49 to $1.99. Again, the owners know they will sell more chicken sandwiches because the price is lower. But they notice that while the chicken sandwich special is running, the quantity of hamburger falls from 650 to 475. Plug these amounts into the formula and we get:

$$P_{Y1} = \$3.49$$
$$Q_{X1} = 650$$
$$P_{Y2} = \$1.99$$
$$Q_{X2} = 475$$

$$E_c = \frac{47 - 650}{1.99 - 3.4} \times \frac{1.99 - 3.49}{475 + 650} = \frac{175}{-1.5} \times \frac{5.48}{1125} = \frac{-959}{-1687.5} = +0.57$$

The first thing you might notice about these two calculations is that while the first result (the calculation with fries and soda pop) is negative—like the own price elasticity calculated earlier—the second one (the calculation with chicken sandwiches and hamburgers) is positive. Remember that an own price elasticity will never be positive because of the negative relationship between a commodity's price and the quantity consumers want. With related goods, however, the direction of the quantity change depends upon what the relationship between the two goods is—complements or substitutes. In the case of complements (fries and soda pop), when the price of one good decreases, the demand for a good that is used with it increases, along with the quantity of the original good. In other words, the cross price relationship is also negative. In the case of substitutes (chicken sandwiches and hamburgers), when the price of a good decreases, consumers will lean toward that substitute good and away from other options available to them.

So, when the price of French fries falls, consumers will want more fries, but they will also want more of the other things they consume with fries, like soda pop. The price of fries goes down, causing an increase in the demand for pop, creates a negative relationship. Because of this negative relationship, we see that the result of the cross-price elasticity computation is negative. In the other example, when the price of a chicken sandwich falls, consumers will want more chicken sandwiches, but they will also want fewer hamburgers. The price of chicken sandwiches falls, causing a decrease in the demand for hamburgers, creates a positive relationship. It should be no surprise, then, that the number we get from the cross-price elasticity computation is positive.

The plus or minus signs of the cross-price elasticities thus depend on whether the goods are complements (minus sign) or substitutes (plus sign). But what about the magnitude of the number? Basically this tells us the same thing as the own price elasticity result does. The cross-price elasticity between fries and soda pop is -0.99. This means that if the price of fries falls by 10 percent, the demand for soda pop will increase by 9.9 percent. Of course, it also means that if the price of fries increases by 10 percent, the demand for soda pop will decrease by 9.9 percent. The cross-price elasticity between chicken sandwiches and hamburgers is +0.57. Therefore, if the price of chicken sandwiches is lowered by 10 percent, consumers will buy 5.7 percent fewer hamburgers. Likewise, if the price of chicken sandwiches goes up by 10 percent, consumers will buy 5.7 percent more hamburgers. Another thing these computations reveal is a difference in the strength of product relationships: Fries and soda pop appear to be more strongly related than chicken sandwiches and hamburgers.

Businesses find cross-price elasticities very helpful in predicting what effect a competitor's price change will have on their own products. Pricing complementary goods (razors and razor blades, for example) is much easier if the seller knows how consumers respond to change in the price of one of these goods. In fact, it is common for a good to be priced very low (sometimes at a loss) because the business knows that if consumers increase their demand for that good, they will also buy more of a complementary good—which is priced much higher. Razors, for example, are very cheap, so consumers will buy a lot of razors. However,

TABLE 3.4

Cross Price Elasticity Examples

Goods	Elasticity
Butter and margarine	+0.81
Beef and pork	+0.28
Razors and razor blades	−2.42

razor blades (a complement) are relatively expensive. Because consumers use them together, businesses can actually lose money on the manufacture and sale of razors, knowing that they will make it up in the sale of the blades.

INCOME ELASTICITY

In addition to a good's own price and the price of related goods, one of the other major determinants of demand for that good is how much income consumers have. Recall from Chapter 2 that the direction of the quantity changes depends on price but also upon what type of good it is. For normal goods, the more income a consumer has, the greater the demand for these goods; likewise, the less income a consumer has, the smaller the demand. In other words, income and demand have a positive relationship—they both go up or they both go down. For inferior goods, the opposite is true. When consumer income increases, demand for inferior goods falls; as consumer income decreases, demand increases (a negative relationship). We can measure the extent to which demand changes as a result of income changes by computing an **income elasticity**:

Income Elasticity of Demand:

$$E_1 = \frac{\text{Percentage change in Q}}{\text{Percentage change in I}}$$

Formula for Computing Income Elasticity of Demand:

$$E_1 = \frac{Q_2 - Q_1}{I_2 - I_1} \times \frac{I_2 + I_1}{Q_2 + Q_1}$$

Notice that the format of these equations is exactly the same as for the other two measures of elasticity (i.e., own price and cross-price). The only difference here is that this time we are measuring the percentage change in the quantity demand of a good when income changes. Also notice that we no longer need to differentiate between goods X and Y. We are looking only at the change of demand in one good.

Let's work through an example. Assume that you have a part-time job and earn $150 per week. One of the reasons you have a part-time job is so you can afford to do things with your friends, especially going to the movies, which you do about once a week. Because you have been a hard worker, your boss gives you a raise and now you earn $180 per week. As a result, you go to the movies more often—now about twice a week. When we put this situation into our formula, we get:

$$I_1 = \$150$$
$$Q_1 = 1$$
$$I_2 = \$180$$
$$Q_2 = 2$$

$$E_I = \frac{2-1}{180-150} \times \frac{180+150}{2+1} = \frac{1}{30} \times \frac{330}{3} = \frac{330}{90} = +3.67$$

Now let's change the situation slightly and get a different measure before we examine what the +3.67 at the end of our equation means. Before you got your raise you were earning $150 per week. You were also consuming about 3 fast-food meals per week. After you got your raise, you stopped eating fast food as often—only once a week—and started going out to nicer restaurants instead. Let's calculate the data in this situation.

$$I_1 = \$150$$
$$Q_1 = 3$$
$$I_2 = \$180$$
$$Q_2 = 1$$

$$E_I = \frac{1-3}{180-150} \times \frac{108+150}{1+3} = \frac{-2}{30} \times \frac{330}{4} = \frac{-660}{120} = -5.5$$

The result from the first equation was +3.67. The result here is −5.5 Both situations involve an increase in your income. In the first case, the increase in income means you can go to the movies more often. It should be no surprise, then, that the income elasticity here is a positive number. Both income and demand are moving in the same direction, leading to a positive measure for income elasticity: +3.67. We would get the same result if income had decreased—you would have cut back on the number of movies, so again, both variables would have moved in the same direction. In the second case, your raise means you can reduce the number of fast-food meals you buy—a negative relationship that is confirmed by a negative income elasticity of –5.5. If income had fallen, the number of fast-food meals would have increased—again, a negative relationship. So, for normal goods, the income elasticity is reflected by a positive number. For inferior goods, it is reflected by a negative number.

As with the other measures of elasticity, the magnitude of the number derived from the computation(s) indicates the strength of consumer responsiveness. In the first case, if income increases by 10 percent, demand (movies) will increase by 36.7 percent. In the second case, if income increases by 10 percent, demand (fast-food meals) will decrease by 55 percent. Both measures reveal that consumer demand for movies and fast-food meals is very sensitive to changes in income.

OTHER MEASURES OF ELASTICITY

It should be clear by this point that there is nothing magical or mysterious about elasticities—in fact, the formulas are very predictable. They are simply measures of how quantity demanded of a particular good changes when something else changes. That something else can be the good's own price, the price of another good, consumer income—or other factors, such as advertising. It is also possible to measure the elasticity of supply. After all, there is another side to the market, and suppliers respond to changes in various conditions as well. We can measure the strength of those responses using elasticity, just as we did for consumers and the demand side of the market.

Elasticity of demand has a role to play in tax policy. **Excise taxes** are taxes that are based on how many units are sold. So, rather than the tax being based

TABLE 3.5
Examples of Income Elasticities

Goods	Elasticity
Restaurant meals	+1.40
Automobiles	+2.46
Public Transportation	−0.36
Margarine	−0.20

on the total sale (price × quantity), an excise tax is a unit tax (only quantity). Which good do you think it more likely to have an excise tax placed on it: gasoline or milk? Cigarettes or gum? Liquor or cereal? If you said the first good in each of these pairs, you are right. Why? Because consumers are not likely to be very responsive to price changes with these goods. For most consumers gasoline is a necessity. Cigarettes and liquor have few (or no) substitutes. In each case, there are few (or no) substitutes. If consumers are not especially price sensitive, the price of each of these commodities can be increased (with a tax) without much affect on quantity demanded.

When the government decides to impose excise taxes, price elasticity is an important consideration. But sometimes the government gets it wrong. As part of the 1990 budget, President Bush's administration levied a 10 percent luxury tax on big-ticket items ($100,000 or more), such as yachts, private jets, and furs. The reasoning behind this was that people who had enough money to afford these things would not be very sensitive to the tax price increase, and thus the government could increase its tax revenues. Apparently no one involved in this reasoning computed the elasticities involved. When the excise tax on yachts was imposed, the quantity demanded of yachts dropped precipitously. As a result of the 10 percent price increase, those in the market for a yacht either changed their minds and did not buy at all, or they bought yachts overseas. As a result, not only did the government not raise much revenue, but tens of thousands of boatyard employees were laid off as U.S. yacht builders nationwide went out of business. Thus the government assumption that the demand for yachts was inelastic led to some dire consequences. The luxury tax was repealed in 1993.

SUMMARY

Understanding the basic demand and supply relationships is good, but understanding the strength and causes of these relationships is very important. Numerous examples provided in this chapter illustrated these factors; here we will answer a question posed in the opening paragraph: Why are last-minute Broadway show tickets so cheap, while last-minute airline tickets are so expensive? Part of the answer will come from your own knowledge base and reasoning skills. Part will be based on concepts discussed in this chapter.

Here's a starting point: Think about the motivations of the consumers buying each kind of ticket. If you are buying a last-minute airline ticket, it is probably because you really need to get somewhere. You have a family emergency, or you need to travel suddenly because of your job—some reason that necessitates you getting someplace quickly. In other words, your responsiveness to ticket prices is going to be very slight—your elasticity of demand is small. On the other hand, if you are thinking of buying last-minute Broadway show tickets, there is not as much urgency or necessity involved. You have other options available to you because there are a lot of other things you can do in New York

City besides going to a Broadway show, and it is not imperative that you see one. Thus your responsiveness to price is going to be quite high, meaning your elasticity of demand will be larger.

Much of this chapter dealt with answering the question of how much quantity changes when price changes. This chapter and the previous one emphasize the importance of an underlying principle that affects all consumers in all market transactions: choice.

Further Reading

Arnold, R.A. *How to Think Like an Economist*. Mason, Ohio: South-Western College Publishing, 2004.

Colander, D. *The Stories Economists Tell*. New York: McGraw-Hill, 2005.

Heyne, P., P.J. Boettke, and D.L. Prychitko. *The Economic Way of Thinking*. New York: Prentice Hall, 2009.

Jevons, M. *Murder at the Margin*. Princeton, N.J.: Princeton University Press, 1993.

———. *Fatal Equilibrium*. Greenwich, Conn.: Fawcett Publishing, 1986.

Levitt, S.J., and S.J. Dubner. *Freakonomics: A Rogue Economist Explains the Hidden Side of Everything*. New York: HarperCollins, 2005.

———. *Superfreakonomics: Global Cooling, Patriotic Prostitutes, and Why Suicide Bombers Should Buy Life Insurance*. New York: HarperCollins, 2009.

CHAPTER 4

CONSUMER CHOICE

INTRODUCTION

Chapter 2 examined basic demand and supply relationships. Consumers respond to decreasing prices by increasing their quantity demanded; producers respond to the same decreasing prices by reducing their quantity supplied. In Chapter 3, we learned that elasticity measures tell us how much these quantity changes will be. But we still have not addressed the "why" question. Why do consumers demand more when the price falls? Or stated another way, why are consumers only willing to buy more if the price falls? Why does the value consumers place on something fall when the amount they consume increases? This chapter addresses that question; Chapter 5 addresses the parallel question about the supply curve for producers.

HOW TO MEASURE HAPPINESS

When you act as a consumer and purchase something, you do so because you expect that your purchase will bring you pleasure or satisfy a need. It stands to reason that the more of something you buy, the more pleasure or satisfaction you get from it. We call the total amount of happiness or satisfaction you get from consuming something **total utility**. Remember the discussion of marginal decision making from Chapter 1? Here it comes again. When consumers make decisions about what and how much to buy, they do not really think about total utility—they consider **marginal utility**.

Let's look at an example. Suppose you are out with friends and you order several pizzas to share. When the pizzas come, everybody digs in because everyone is starving. That first piece tastes really good, right? The second one tastes pretty good, too. The third piece still tastes great, but your enthusiasm is starting to fade a bit. You eat the fourth piece only because there is still a lot left, and it shouldn't go to waste (you have temporarily forgotten about sunk costs). By now you're getting very full. You eat a fifth piece for reasons that you cannot remember and are very sorry you did. If we attach numbers to this scenario, it might look like the breakdown in Table 4.1.

First, let's talk about the numbers in the total utility column. What does it mean to have 50 total utilities? Absolutely nothing. The size of that number does not matter. What matters is how the rest of the numbers relate to it. The first number could have been 2 or 1,000 or 3 million. What matters is, how large the second number and the third, etc., are, relative to the first. In this case, we see that whatever amount of satisfaction (or happiness or utility) we get from the first piece of pizza, the second one increases our happiness. So does the third one. The fourth one does not, and the fifth one actually detracts from our happiness.

But we know from Chapter 1, that good decisions are not made on the basis of totals. Good decisions are made using marginals. So let's add marginal utility and look at that table again.

This is the same information we had in Table 4.1, but with a column added for marginal utility. Marginal utility is the additional happiness (satisfaction, utility) you get when you consume one more unit of something. Looking at the marginal utility column, we can get a better idea of how your satisfaction changes as you eat your dinner. The first piece of pizza gives you 50 units of utility (again the actual number does not matter). The second piece gives you more

TABLE 4.1
Consumption of Pizza and Total Utility

Slices of Pizza	Total Utility
1	50
2	70
3	85
4	85
5	80

TABLE 4.2
Consumption of Pizza, Total and Marginal Utility

Slices of Pizza	Total Utility	Marginal Utility
1	50	—
2	70	20
3	85	15
4	85	0
5	80	−5

satisfaction (70), meaning that the second piece added to your happiness by 20 units. Likewise, your happiness increases again when you eat the third piece (to 85), or by 15 additional units. The fourth piece does not add to your happiness at all (marginal utility is zero), while the marginal utility of the fifth piece is negative, indicating that your satisfaction decreases with that piece.

If you think about it, you will realize that this pattern is generally true for just about everything you purchase. Initially, your pleasure from consuming something is high, but as you keep consuming it, your satisfaction falls. We can see from our example above that the fourth piece of pizza is consistent with being satiated, and the fifth represents the regret from having eaten too much. This pattern of marginal utility decreasing as more is consumed is called the **law of diminishing marginal utility**.

How does this approach help us understand how consumers make decisions? How many pieces of pizza should you eat? The only thing we know so far is that you definitely should not eat five, and in all likelihood, not four, either. But a more exact answer requires another piece of the puzzle. So far we have only looked at one good—pizza. Of course, we all purchase many more goods and services than one, and we need to balance the satisfaction we get from consuming one relative to the others. How can you balance the marginal utility from one more piece of pizza to the marginal utility derived from one more compact disc, for example? Table 4.3 shows what the utility schedule might be for CDs.

As with pizza, it does not matter what numbers we use for total utility—the important point is that the relationship of total utility to number of CDs is maintained. As the quantity of CDs increases, so does total utility, which is what we would expect. But, as quantity increases, marginal utility falls. Each additional CD contributes less to our happiness than the previous one—diminishing marginal utility.

TABLE 4.3
Consumption of CDs, Total and Marginal Utility

# of CDs	Total Utility	Marginal Utility
1	200	—
2	300	100
3	360	60
4	400	40
5	420	20

Looking at the two goods, however, the marginal utility of one more CD is greater than that of another piece of pizza—so you would buy another CD, right? To use a more extreme case, how about the marginal utility of one more movie compared to one more vacation? As you may have guessed, the piece of the puzzle that is missing is that these things have very different prices.

Recall from Chapter 2 that demand is how much consumers are able and willing to buy at every price. So far in this chapter, we have been looking at willingness to buy. So how much satisfaction something brings you forms the basis of how willing you are to buy it. But what about ability? For that, we need to

TABLE 4.4
Quantities of CDs and Pizza

Combinations of CDs and Pizzas That Total $50	
CDs	Number of Pizzas
0	10
1	8
2	6
3	4
4	2
5	0

know the prices of commodities and how much money we have to spend—our budget. To keep things simple, let's assume that pizzas and CDs are the only two things we can spend our money on. The price of each pizza is $5, and the price of each CD is $10. So if we have $50 to spend, we can buy 10 pizzas, 5 CDs, or some combination of the two. Table 4.4 shows various combinations of pizzas and CDs that match our budget.

Now we know how many CDs and pizzas we are able to buy, but this table does not tell us anything about how many we want to buy. We need to combine the information on willingness to buy (marginal utility) with information about ability to buy (prices and budget) to complete our picture of consumer decisions. Although the marginal utility of another CD is much greater than that of another piece of pizza, so is the price. On the other hand, we do not take the price of something into account to the exclusion of the amount of satisfaction we would get from consuming it. In other words, pizza is cheaper but we don't necessarily want to spend all of our $50 on pizzas because of this—we want some music, too.

Now let's put these two concepts together and see what they tell us about consumer decisions. We already know that choosing the good with the highest marginal utility is not realistic. We also know that choosing the good with the lowest price probably will not increase our happiness by much. A way to incorporate both ability and willingness to buy is to not think about how much marginal utility we get from something relative to another good, but how much marginal utility *per dollar* we get from one good compared to another.

Let's go back to the marginal utility tables we constructed for pizza and CDs. The data from each of these are combined in Table 4.5.

TABLE 4.5
Consumption of CDs and Pizza, Total and Marginal Utility

Slices of Pizza	Total Utility	Marginal Utility	# of CDs	Total Utility	Marginal Utility
1	50	—	1	200	—
2	70	20	2	300	100
3	85	15	3	360	60
4	85	0	4	400	40
5	80	−5	5	420	20

TABLE 4.6

Consumption of CDs and Pizzas,
Total and Marginal Utility Per Dollar

Slices of Pizza	Total Utility	Marginal Utility	Marginal Utility Per Dollar: Pizza	# of CDs	Total Utility	Marginal Utility	Marginal Utility Per Dollar: CDs
1	50	—	—	1	200	—	—
2	70	20	20/5 = 4	2	300	100	100/10 = 10
3	85	15	15/5 = 3	3	360	60	60/10 = 6
4	85	0	0/5 = 0	4	400	40	40/10 = 4
5	80	−5	−5/5 = −1	5	420	20	20/10 = 2

We see that the second piece of pizza increases our happiness by 20 units, whereas the second CD increases it by 100 units. If we were just interested in willingness to buy, we would obviously buy more CDs. But CDs cost a lot more than pizza does—twice as much. Therefore, to incorporate both willingness and ability, we need to see how much additional utility we get per dollar spent on each good. This is presented in Table 4.6.

Table 4.6 shows that the third slice of pizza gets us 3 additional units of happiness for each dollar we spend on pizza. It also shows that the fifth CD gives us 2 additional units of happiness for each dollar we spend on CDs. What if we choose to buy 4 slices of pizza and 3 CDs? We can afford to do that because 4 slices of pizza will cost $20 and 3 CDs will cost $30. So the "able" part of our requirement is met. But what about the "willing" part? The marginal utility per dollar for 4 slices of pizza is 0. The marginal utility per dollar for 3 CDs is 6. If you get more satisfaction per dollar spent on CDs than you do for pizza, what would you do? Buy more CDs, right? But remember, you can't buy CDs without buying fewer pizzas. So let's say you buy another CD. You know your marginal utility of this last CD will be less than marginal utility of the third one (diminishing marginal utility), and the marginal utility per dollar is 4. To buy this fourth CD, you need to buy 2 fewer pizzas, or you need to reduce your consumption of pizza to 2 slices. At that level, your marginal utility per dollar is also 4. If you are getting 4 units of satisfaction per dollar for pizzas *and* CDs, will you change your consumption choice? But if you try other combinations, you see that you will not get more satisfaction per dollar than you do with the 4 CDs–2 pizza slices combination.

Our example uses only two goods to keep things simple, but regardless of how many goods we consume, the combination of goods that maximizes our happiness is where these marginal utilities per dollar are all equal:

$$\frac{MU}{P} = \frac{MU_A}{P_A} = \frac{MU_B}{P_B} = \frac{MU_C}{P_C} =$$

Now we all know that the last time you went to buy something, you definitely did not have this formula running around in your head. But the remarkable thing about consumer choice theory is that you behaved as if you did. Think of it this way. Let's say you play tennis. When you serve, do you think to yourself, "First, I'm going to contract my shoulder, then I'm going to contract my lat muscles, now I'm going to work my hip flexors . . ."? Of course you don't. But to someone observing you, it may look like you do. In other words, when you do something that works your muscles, you do not consciously think about doing so, but you behave as if you do. Consumer behavior works the same way—you do not consciously think about equating the marginal utility per dollar spent on each thing you buy. But you act as if you do. Economists studying consumer behavior report remarkably consistent and predictable results that conform to this model.

So now we know how people make consumption decisions—even though they make those decisions without even realizing it! But what about the demand curve? Why are consumers only willing to buy more of something if its price falls? Because the more of something you have, the less utility you get from each additional unit—diminishing marginal utility. The demand curve slopes down because as quantity increases, you value each unit less and less. If you value something less, you are only willing to buy it if its price is also falling.

SUMMARY

In Chapter 2, we learned the basics of the demand function, which shows a negative relationship between the price of something and the quantity that consumers want of it. And while it seems intuitive that a lower price would lead consumers to buy more and a higher price would lead consumers to buy less, there really is a lot more to the demand relationship than this simplistic explanation. The fuller explanation of the relationship is grounded in the law of diminishing marginal utility—how much value we place on subsequent units. Because that value falls, so does the price we are willing to pay. Similarly, the way in which consumers make their purchasing decisions across everything that they buy is grounded in equating marginal utility per dollar of each good.

Your purchasing decisions closely conform to consumer choice theory—without you even being aware of it!

Further Reading

Ariely, D. *Predictably Irrational: The Hidden Forces That Shape Our Decisions.* New York: HarperCollins, 2008.

———. *The Upside of Irrationality: The Unexpected Benefits of Defying Logic & Work and at Home.* New York: HarperCollins, 2010.

Jevons, M. *A Deadly Indifference: A Henry Spearman Mystery.* Princeton, N.J.: Princeton University Press, 1995.

Lindstrom, M. *Buyology: Truth and Lies About Why We Buy.* New York: Random House, 2008.

Schwartz, B. *The Paradox of Choice: Why More Is Less.* New York: HarperCollins, 2004.

CHAPTER 5

PRODUCTION AND COST

INTRODUCTION

In Chapter 4, we drew the curtain back on the demand curve to discover what really makes the demand curve have a negative slope. We are going to do the same thing for the supply curve. It makes intuitive sense that the higher the price, the more producers are willing to provide to the market. But as in the case of demand, there is more to this than a single, simple explanation. Along the way, we will address a variety of topics having to do with businesses' decisions about how to use resources. Some are obvious; others are less so. For example, why do drive-through ATMs have Braille on the keypads? What you learn from this chapter answers this and similar questions about production and cost that influence the supply curve.

SHORT RUN VS. LONG RUN

Businesses make many decisions about how much to produce and how to produce within the context of two timeframes. The first of these timeframes is the **short run**. In economic terms, this is often not a specific period of time; it varies from company to company. What is true for all companies, however, is that the short run is the period of time when at least one of the **inputs** is **fixed**. Inputs are the resources companies use to produce the **output**—whatever good or service they happen to make. To make things simple, we'll focus on the two most important inputs: **labor** and **capital**. Labor refers to the workers, and capital refers to plant and equipment. In the short run, capital is fixed. For example, if a business is operating one plant, it cannot suddenly open a new plant—this takes time to build or acquire. Likewise, a business cannot buy a new piece of equipment quickly. Sometimes that process has to be bid out; sometimes the equipment takes time to be constructed and delivered—in either case, it is a process that takes longer than a few days or weeks. On the other hand, labor can be changed very quickly. Workers can be hired or fired in a matter of hours or days. Therefore, labor is a **variable** input of production in the short run.

The second timeframe is the long run. In the **long run**, businesses can build or buy a new plant and place orders for new equipment. Essentially, there are no fixed inputs in the long run—everything is variable. The long run is typically viewed as more of a planning timeframe. In the short run, a business tries to do the best it can with what it currently has to work with. In the long run, the business takes a different view: In the next year or two or three, what do we want our company to look like? How many plants should we have? How much equipment? The long-run view allows companies to make changes to the current fixed inputs to achieve their objectives. The short-run view involves the company trying to do the best it can with what it has.

Any production process involves certain costs. These costs are related to the fixed and variable inputs described above. The short run is defined as a period of time in which at least one input cannot be changed, for example, capital. The costs of the fixed input(s) are called **fixed costs**. Fixed costs do not change in the short run, and they are not related to how much is produced. For example, businesses have to pay insurance and make payments on loans or other contractual obligations even if they do not produce anything. And these payments will not change until the insurance policy is up for renewal or until the loan or other obligation is paid off. On the other hand, **variable costs** do depend on how much is produced, and they are associated with the variable input. When businesses produce more, they use more raw materials, labor, electricity, etc. Variable costs are the costs of these and similar inputs; they change in the short run and also determine how much is produced.

One final note about costs. When economists talk about the costs of production, they are referring to all the costs of production, both **explicit** and **implicit**. Explicit costs are those costs that are covered when money actually changes hands. Worker salaries, utilities, loan payments, invoices are all explicit costs of doing business. Implicit costs are what we have previously referred to as opportunity costs. No money changes hands with opportunity costs. Instead, these costs represent foregone opportunities for the business. For example, if the business sells some of its investments so that it has enough capital to build a new plant, the explicit costs would include the cost of purchasing the land, constructing the building, etc. The implicit or opportunity cost is the return the investments could have provided had they not been sold. As we go forward, assume that "cost" includes both explicit and implicit costs.

PRODUCTION IN THE SHORT RUN

Let's say you want to bake some cookies. You get out the mixing bowl and the beaters and turn on the oven. You mix together some flour, eggs, flavorings, and other ingredients and make dough. Then you put the dough on the cookie sheets and put your cookies in the oven to bake. You know how to mix all these things together because the recipe tells you how much of each ingredient to use. But what if you want to double the number of cookies you produce? You can increase the inputs by doubling the ingredients. But it's going to take you longer to produce more cookies because you have only a certain number of cookie sheets and only one oven. In other words, your capital is fixed. It's unlikely you would run out and buy more cookie sheets or another oven to increase production.

Companies also have to come up with their own "recipes" of how to combine labor, raw materials and other inputs to produce something. They take some combination of inputs, put them together, and produce an output, just like you do when you bake cookies. But when companies want to increase output in the short run, they face the same dilemma you face when you have a limited number of cookie sheets and a single oven. If they want to increase output in the short run, all they can do is increase their variable inputs. They are stuck with the fixed inputs they have, at least for the time being.

When you make cookies, your recipe includes several inputs. To make things easy, we will assume that companies have only two inputs: labor (variable in the short run) and capital (fixed in the short run). Companies combine labor and capital to produce an output, Q, according to some "recipe" or function, so

$$Q = f(L, K)$$

where "f" refers to function, L refers to the number of workers and K refers to capital. (Note: Economists *do* know how to spell capital. "K" is used to represent "capital" in microeconomics because "C" is used as the abbreviation for "consumption" in macroeconomics.)

Following this equation, businesses combine labor and capital in ways that vary with what it is they are producing. For example, clothing manufacturing is a very labor-intensive industry. It involves some capital (sewing machines), but relies heavily on human capital. On the other hand, automobile manufacturing is a very capital intensive process. Certainly workers are involved, but the amount and complexity of equipment used in the process makes the labor/capital mix much different from what we have in clothing manufacturing.

One additional note about the production function defined above is that output is denoted by "Q." This is the same "Q" we used when discussing demand and supply in Chapter 2, and it represents "quantity." What we are working toward in this chapter is explaining why the quantity that producers are willing to provide to the market increases with price. So the quantity involved with the supply curve and the market in general, is the same quantity that a firm produces with its inputs.

Regardless of the specific way in which companies mix labor and capital, all companies share some commonalities in the short run. We can illustrate what these commonalities are by using an example. Assume that our business produces shirts. In the short run, we must use the amount of capital that we already have—the plant, the number of sewing machines, the cutting tables, pairs of scissors—all these pieces of capital are fixed in the short run. The only thing we can change in the short run is how many workers we have working with this capital. Table 5.1 shows the number of shirts that can be produced with varying amounts of labor.

There are several things to notice about this table. First, we see that (as expected) the more workers we hire, the greater the number of shirts we can produce—at least up until the eighth worker. (We'll talk about this exception later.) We also see that if we hire the first worker, that worker can produce 4 shirts. If we hire the second worker, the total number of shirts we can produce increases to 9. This must mean that the second worker adds 5 shirts to total production. If we hire 3 workers, our total production increases to 16. If two workers produced 9 shirts and three workers produced 16 shirts, this must mean that

TABLE 5.1
Number of Workers and Total Product

# of Workers (L)	# of Shirts Produced (Q)
0	0
1	4
2	9
3	16
4	22
5	26
6	28
7	28
8	25

TABLE 5.2
Number of Workers, Total and Marginal Product

# of Workers (L)	# of Shirts Produced (Q)	Marginal Product (MP)
0	0	—
1	4	4
2	9	5
3	16	7
4	22	6
5	26	4
6	28	2
7	28	0
8	25	−3

the third worker added 7 shirts to the total production. These additional shirts produced by each worker is called the **marginal product of labor.** The marginal product, or MP, is the additional output that is produced by adding one more worker. If we add another column to our table, we can see marginal product more clearly.

In Table 5.2 we can see that the marginal product of the third worker is 7. In other words, two workers produced 9 shirts and 3 workers produced 16 shirts, so the difference of 7 is attributed to the third worker. Notice that as more workers are added to the production process (up to 3 workers), marginal product increases. So not only is each additional worker adding more to output, but each worker is adding an increasing amount to output. Why?

The simple answer to this question is that marginal product increases because workers specialize. In our shirt example, if only one worker is hired, that one worker has to cut the material, sew the seams, sew on the buttons, and do everything else required. If we hire two workers, one can do all the cutting while the other does all the sewing. If we hire three workers, one can cut, one can sew the seams, and the third can sew on the buttons. When workers specialize, everyone becomes more productive and marginal product increases.

But look what happens with the fourth worker. The marginal product of that worker is 6. When we hire this worker, our shirt output continues to increase, but by only 6 shirts whereas the third worker caused output to

Assembly lines (such as this one in an automobile industry) require workers to specialize in one task. This greatly reduces the time and cost required to produce each unit. *(Shutterstock)*

increase by 7 shirts. It gets worse. The marginal product of the fifth worker is only 4, and that of the sixth is only 2. Output is still increasing, but not as much as it increased when we hired the second and third worker. When we hire the sixth worker, for example, output went from 26 shirts to 28 shirts, meaning the output of that worker was only 2 additional shirts. This pattern is called **diminishing marginal product** or **diminishing returns to labor**. In other words, eventually, the last worker we hire will produce fewer units than the person hired before him or her produced. In this example, diminishing returns sets in after the third worker is hired. Although the total number of shirts produced has increased, the increase attributed to worker 4 is not as high as that attributed to worker 3.

This pattern should be familiar to you—it was something introduced in Chapter 4 while discussing diminishing marginal utility. This is the same concept, except that in this chapter, it is being applied to production instead of consumption. So both sides of the market, demand and supply, are affected by a similar sort of process and constraints.

One important thing to note is that the situation described here is not a reflection on labor quality. The reason we have diminishing marginal product is not that the workers are incapable or that they are not working hard; the reason is that we are operating in the short run. This means we have a fixed amount of plant and equipment, and when we keep adding workers to a fixed space and fixed machinery, their productivity will eventually start to fall. Let's look at what is likely to happen in the scenario we have created.

In our example, all of our workers have equal ability and can specialize in different activities. This is efficient and speeds things up. So why does marginal product fall after the third worker? Because we are operating in the short run. We have fixed capital. The plant and equipment stay the same. And although having workers specialize increases marginal product, the fixed capital cannot sustain this pattern of specialization. We already have the first worker cutting fabric, the second worker sewing seams, and the third worker doing hand sewing. If we hire a fourth worker, what will that worker do? Because of fixed capital, we have only one cutting table and one sewing machine. The fourth worker could help with the cutting (assuming we have another pair of scissors), so output might still increase, but not as much as it did with the third worker. When worker number 5 comes in, he/she could also help with the cutting, but it is starting to get a little crowded. Worker number 6 could run the cut fabric over to the sewing machine operator and then to the hand-sewer, but things are really getting crowded—fixed capital means we have not expanded the facility we started with, so we have limited space and now we have 6 workers packed into it. When we hire worker number 7, total output does not change—so the marginal product of that last worker is 0. And if we hire worker number 8, things are so crowded that the workers are getting in each other's way (and on each others' nerves) to such an extent that total output actually falls—8 workers produce less than 7 workers did.

If we could snap our fingers and create more space, more sewing machines, and more cutting tables, we could keep adding workers and not experience diminishing marginal product. But in the short run, we are stuck with the plant and equipment we currently have, so we will always have diminishing returns.

Costs in the Short Run

In our shirt manufacturing example, the variable costs of production include wages paid to workers, the costs of cloth, thread, electricity—the more shirts we make, the greater the costs of these inputs. The costs of the sewing machine and the cutting table are fixed and cannot be changed in the short run, even if we decided not to produce any shirts. Let's assume that the cost of the sewing machine and the table are $50 and that the wage for each additional worker is $60. In Table 5.3 we expand our previous production table to include costs.

TABLE 5.3
Level of Production and Costs

# of Workers (L)	# of Shirts Produced (Q)	Marginal Product (MP)	Fixed Costs (FC)	Variable Costs (VC)	Total Costs (TC)
0	0	—	$50	$0	$50
1	4	4	$50	$60	$110
2	9	5	$50	$120	$170
3	16	7	$50	$180	$230
4	22	6	$50	$240	$290
5	26	4	$50	$300	$350
6	28	2	$50	$360	$410
7	28	0	$50	$420	$470

The first thing you should notice is that we have omitted the row that showed what happens with eight workers. As you saw in Table 5.2, that eighth worker moves us into negative marginal product. No business would choose to produce at that level, so we will limit this table to seven workers. Now let's look at the column for fixed costs. These are costs for inputs (the sewing machine and the table) and remain constant (at $50)—all the way down. Those inputs do not change, and therefore, the costs associated with them do not change either. If we produce zero shirts, our fixed costs are $50. If we produce 1,000 shirts, our fixed costs are still $50. Now look at the next column, under variable costs. Here you see that the more we produce, the higher our costs are. As we add workers, our variable costs increase by $60 per worker—regardless of how much the worker produces. The last column, total costs, is simply the sum of fixed and variable costs.

Table 5.3 provides quite a bit of information, but we're still missing some vital data. We have a good idea of the costs associated with input, but before deciding how many shirts we should produce, we also need to know the costs associated with our level of output. That means we need to add more columns to our table.

You may be thinking that our table is starting to look a little intimidating, but we haven't changed very much. The last three columns all are simply averages of the things discussed—the result of dividing the cost by the quantity. So to get the average fixed cost, we divide fixed cost by quantity. For example, the average fixed cost of producing 16 units of output (or 16 shirts) is $3.13 ($50/16). The average fixed cost of producing 26 units of output is $1.92 ($50/26). Average variable cost is computed the same way. On average, 22 units of output cost $10.91 in variable costs ($240/22). The last column simply sums average fixed and average variable costs to get average total costs.

If you look down the columns, you see that fixed cost steadily declines. This should make sense to you—fixed costs do not change, but as we add workers, output increases. That makes average fixed costs fall over the whole range of workers and output. Average variable costs and average total costs look different, however. Notice that initially both of these values decrease. Eventually however, both begin to increase. We will explain why this occurs later in the chapter, but first we'll continue to analyze the data we have so far.

The average costs give us important information about our production decision. Would you ever want to produce something at a level that meant your average costs would not be covered by the price you got for your output? Obviously not. Now let's apply this to our example by turning the shirt business over to you. What if the selling price of your shirts were $30, and you were producing 16 shirts (assume for the time being that 16 shirts is the

TABLE 5.4
Levels of Production and Average Costs

(L)	(Q)	Marginal Product (MP)	Fixed Costs (FC)	Variable Costs (VC)	Total Costs (TC)	Average Fixed Costs (AFC)	Average Variable Costs (AVC)	Average Total Costs (ATC)
0	0	—	$50	$0	$50	—	—	—
1	4	4	$50	$60	$110	$12.50	$15.00	$27.50
2	9	5	$50	$120	$170	$5.56	$13.33	$18.89
3	16	7	$50	$180	$230	$3.13	$11.25	$14.38
4	22	6	$50	$240	$290	$2.27	$10.91	$13.18
5	26	4	$50	$300	$350	$1.92	$11.54	$13.46
6	28	2	$50	$360	$410	$1.79	$12.86	$14.65
7	28	0	$50	$420	$470	$1.79	$15.00	$16.79

"best" level of production for you—we'll discuss what this means in Chapter 6). Would you do this? Of course, you would. The total cost per shirt (ATC) at 16 units of production is $14.38, so if you were getting $30 per shirt, you would be making a nice profit of $15.62 per shirt. But what if you were producing 16 shirts and the price of a shirt were only $14? Would you continue to produce 16 shirts? The total cost per shirt at 16 units of production is $14.38, so a price of $14 would not cover your average total costs of production. Would you still produce 16 shirts?

If you answered "no", think again. You would continue to produce! Surprised? Here's why. At a price of $14, you are not covering the average cost, but you are covering the average variable costs, which are $11.25. Why is that enough? Because you have two options. You can continue to produce 16 shirts (because that is the best output level), or you can decide that the price is too low and get out of the shirt producing business all together—produce zero.

In the short run, if you decide to produce 16 shirts, you must pay both fixed and variable costs—you pay for insurance as well as pay for cloth, for example. If you decide not to produce anything, do you avoid all these costs? No, you do not. Remember that the definition of fixed costs are those that you have to pay even if you do not produce anything—they do not vary with production. So, if you decide to produce zero units of output, you still are faced with paying your fixed costs. In both cases—produce or not produce—you must pay fixed costs in the short run. Because you have to pay them regardless of which option you choose, they become irrelevant.

The only costs that remain a consideration, therefore, are variable costs. If you are covering your variable costs of production, you should continue to produce—in the short run. Obviously, you cannot indefinitely continue earning a price that covers only your variable costs—something has to change or you will eventually go out of business. But in the short run, covering your average variable costs is enough.

There is one more cost concept that will be very important in the next chapter when we talk about the "best" quantity to produce—**marginal cost**. As with all other marginal concepts, marginal cost is what happens when there is a change of one. In this case, marginal cost tells us how much costs change when we produce one more unit (that is, one more shirt). In Table 5.5, we add marginal cost to the production and cost table presented above.

Before we consider the usefulness of marginal cost, let's look at how the values in the last column are generated. When we go from the first row to the second row (hiring one worker and producing 4 shirts), costs increase from $50 to $110. So why isn't marginal cost $60 instead of $15? Remember that the definition of marginal cost is the additional cost of producing *one* more unit—$60 is the cost of producing *4* more units. So if $60 is the additional cost we incur if we produce 4 more units, the cost of producing one more unit is $15 ($60/4).

TABLE 5.5
Levels of Production, Average and Marginal Costs

(L)	(Q)	Marginal Product (MP)	Fixed Costs (FC)	Variable Costs (VC)	Total Costs (TC)	Average Fixed Costs (AFC)	Average Variable Costs (AVC)	Average Total Costs (ATC)	Marginal Cost (MC)
0	0	—	$50	$0	$50	—	—	—	—
1	4	4	$50	$60	$110	$12.50	$15.00	$27.50	$15.00
2	9	5	$50	$120	$170	$5.56	$13.33	$18.89	$12.00
3	16	7	$50	$180	$230	$3.13	$11.25	$14.38	$8.57
4	22	6	$50	$240	$290	$2.27	$10.91	$13.18	$10.00
5	26	4	$50	$300	$350	$1.92	$11.54	$13.46	$15.00
6	28	2	$50	$360	$410	$1.79	$12.86	$14.65	$30.00
7	28	0	$50	$420	$470	$1.79	$15.00	$16.79	—

Likewise, going from the second to the third row, we have hired another worker, so costs have increased by $60 again. But again, that's not marginal cost. It is, however, the additional cost of producing 5 more shirts, so if we want the marginal cost of producing just one more, it is $60/5 or $12. Notice that to get marginal cost, we simply divide the change in variable cost (in our case, $60) by the marginal product:

$$MC = \text{Change in VC/MP}$$

It is here that we come back to one of the questions posed in the introduction to this chapter: Why does the supply curve have a positive slope? The answer has several components. First, a positive slope means that producers are only willing to supply more units to the market if the market price increases, reflecting their increasing costs of producing. So the question really becomes, why do marginal costs increase as the number of units produced increases? The first answer is simply a mathematical one. If you look at the formula above for marginal cost, you see that as marginal product falls (the denominator), marginal cost increases. But there is a second, more intuitive answer. Remember what diminishing marginal product means. As we add workers, the last one produces less than the one before. So output is falling with each additional worker. But as we add workers, variable costs are going up by a constant amount—the wage of the worker ($60 in our case). The change in variable costs remain constant at $60, whereas the output we get for that $60 is decreasing. So the cost of producing one more unit must be increasing—we are getting less bang for our buck with each worker we hire, even though that worker still costs us the same as all the other workers. Therefore, just as the demand curve slopes downward because of diminishing marginal utility, the supply curve slopes upward because of diminishing marginal product.

In Chapter 6, which covers market structures, we will be revisiting this marginal cost concept frequently. Although it is interesting to know what is behind the shape of the basic demand and supply curves, the real value of these curves lies in using them to make decisions. In the next chapter we will examine how businesses use the demand and supply curves to decide what that "best" quantity to produce is.

PRODUCTION AND COSTS IN THE LONG RUN

In the long run, there are two important questions businesses must address: What is the optimal number of plants we should be operating? and What is the optimal quantity of pieces of equipment? In other words, when all inputs are variable, what is the best **scale**, or size of operation? In the case of our shirt manufacturing example, we need to decide how many cutting tables and how many sewing machines we need as well as how much space to allocate to making shirts. We can compute how many shirts we can produce if we have a certain amount of space, one table, and one sewing machine. We can also compute how many shirts we can produce if we have two cutting tables, two sewing machines, and double the space. You should recognize that this is a separate, short-run problem, just with inputs fixed at a level that is twice as high as our starting point. We could create another short-run problem by tripling the inputs: three tables, etc. Each one of these is a separate short-run problem with the fixed inputs set at one, two, and three (or more) of table, machine, and space. So, which scale is best? If the long run is the planning period, how do we know what level of plant and equipment is the best?

If you look back at Table 5.5, you see that at an output level of 22 units, we will minimize our average total costs. So if our scale is 1 table, 1 machine and 1 space, the output that minimizes our average costs is 22 shirts. Now assume that we double our scale (2 tables, 2 machines, 2 spaces) and go through the same process of generating a table with production and cost, thus finding the output that minimized average total cost. Let's say that output level is 50 shirts. If we triple our inputs (3 tables, 3 machines, and 3 spaces), our output will, of course, increase again and we can generate all the various production and cost values

TABLE 5.6
Levels of Output with Varying Scale

Scale of Inputs	Output Minimizing Average Total Cost
1 table, 1 machine, 1 space	22 shirts
2 tables, 2 machines, 2 spaces	50 shirts
3 tables, 3 machines, 3 spaces	68 shirts
4 tables, 4 machines, 4 spaces	88 shirts
5 tables, 5 machines, 5 spaces	103 shirts

associated with this level of inputs. Assume that an output level of 68 shirts will minimize our average total costs of production if we triple our size. Table 5.6 presents these combinations of inputs and average cost minimizing output levels.

You should again recognize that each row of this table represents a short-run problem. If we have 4 units of our "fixed" inputs, we are in a short-run situation: What's the best we can do with that scale? If we only have 2 of everything, what is the best we can do with that scale? So looking *across* the table gives us information about various short-run scenarios.

But looking *down* the table gives us information about the long run. What output level should we be planning for? Take a look at the scale, compared to the output levels above. If we double our plant and equipment (from 1 to 2), what happens to output? It increases from 22 shirts to 50 shirts. In other words, it *more* than doubles. If we triple our scale, output increases from 22 to 68—again it *more* than triples. When we are in this situation, we say we are experiencing **increasing returns to scale** or **economies of scale**—when we increase the inputs by some factor (doubling or tripling, for example), our output increases by more than that amount. How can that be?

It seems like magic, but the answer is based on logic not magic. There are several reasons that increasing returns to scale exist. For example, if we can buy some of our inputs in bulk, we can produce a greater quantity at lower average cost. If we produce just a few shirts (and therefore, buy only a small amount of cloth), our average costs will be fairly high. But if we increase production (and buy a larger quantity of cloth, getting a volume discount), we can increase production while experiencing a lower cost per unit. We can also achieve increasing returns to scale if our managerial staff specializes. As we get bigger, we can have cutting managers and sewing managers, rather than one person supervising all activities. This, too, will lower our costs per unit. We may also be able to get a lower interest rate if we finance a larger amount of money (for 4 tables and 4 machines, for example). This would lower our costs per unit.

If we continue looking down the table, we see that if we multiply our inputs by four, output increases by the same factor (from 22 to 88). This is called **constant returns to scale**—when inputs are increased by some multiply and output increases by the same number. Not all production processes have constant returns to scale—a range of output where average costs per unit do not change.

Finally, notice that if we increase our inputs by a multiple of 5, output increases from 22 to 103—less than a factor of five. This is called **diseconomies of scale** or **decreasing returns to scale.** As we continue to increase output, adding tables, machines, and space, we start experiencing an increase in the costs per unit. This typically happens when a business gets too big. In order to manage this very large enterprise, a layer of management must be added to oversee operations, adding to our costs per unit.

So what level of output and, therefore, capital is the best for us in the long run? If we can increase output and enjoy falling average costs, we should certainly do so. But we definitely do not want to produce so much output (requiring so much capital) that our costs per unit increase as we increase output. So for the long term, we should plan on acquiring no more than 4 tables, 4 sewing machines, and 4 spaces.

With this information, we can now address the second question we posed at the beginning of this chapter: Why do drive-through ATMs have Braille on the keypads? The answer lies in the concept of economies of scale. From the standpoint of the business that produces the keypads, it is cheaper (lower cost per unit) to produce a large quantity that is all the same. If this business produced some keypads with Braille and other keypads without Braille, the quantity produced of each type would be smaller, and costs per unit would be higher. Therefore, while it seems illogical to put Braille on drive-through ATM keypads (obviously blind people don't drive), it makes perfect economic sense.

SUMMARY

The decisions facing businesses about how much they produce can examined within two different contexts: the short run and the long run. While businesses are constrained in the short run by their level of capital, in the long run they can make plans to add more capital, or divest themselves of plant and equipment if they have too much. The presence of diminishing marginal product forms the basis for the market supply curve, completing our "behind the scenes" look at the two sides of the market.

Further Reading

Harford, T. *The Logic of Life: The Rational Economics of an Irrational World.* New York: Random House, 2009.

Landsburg, S.E. *Armchair Economist: Economics and Everyday Life.* New York: The Free Press, 1993.

Levitt, S.J., and S.J. Dubner. *Freakonomics: A Rogue Economist Explains the Hidden Side of Everything.* New York: HarperCollins, 2005.

———. *Superfreakonomics: Global Cooling, Patriotic Prostitutes, and Why Suicide Bombers Should Buy Life Insurance.* New York: HarperCollins, 2009.

Milgrom, P., and J. Roberts. *Economics, Organization, and Management.* New York: Prentice Hall, 1992.

Thaler, R.H., and C.R. Sunstein. *Nudge: Improving Decisions About Health, Wealth and Happiness.* New Haven, Conn. Yale University Press, 2008.

Wheelan, C. *The Naked Economics: Undressing the Dismal Science.* New York: W. W. Norton, 2009.

CHAPTER 6

MARKET STRUCTURES

INTRODUCTION

Chapter 5 examined how businesses make their production decisions. A major component of that decision-making process is cost structure. But businesses look at more than cost when deciding how much to produce. What is the "best" output for a business to produce when they look at both sides of the market? How does a firm's competitive environment impact its decisions? This chapter looks at four major market structures and explores how firms behave in each one.

THE FIRM'S OBJECTIVE

In economics, the definition of "best" output is that level of production that maximizes a firm's **profit**. Profit is defined as total revenue minus total costs:

$$\text{Profit} = \text{Total Revenue} - \text{Total Cost}$$

Recall that total revenue is simply the dollar amount of sales (price × quantity). It is especially important to remember that total costs include opportunity cost. So the total cost of a firm refers to all the costs that are covered by a transfer of money *and* opportunity costs—what the firm gave up in order to be in business at all.

The goal of profit maximization may not be true for every firm at all times, but it is true most of the time for all firms. To simplify, let's assume that the primary goal of firms is to maximize their profit. So if a firm's goal is to maximize profit, that firm must take both demand and supply into account. You can see both sides of the market in the formula given above. The demand side of the market is reflected in total revenue—price and quantity. The supply side of the market is reflected in total costs, as covered in the previous chapter. In order to maximize profit, a firm could go through a trial-and-error process of choosing a quantity, finding total revenue and total costs at that quantity, doing the same thing with another quantity, and so on until finding the greatest difference between revenue and costs. But this is a very cumbersome and inefficient process. Luckily there is a better one.

In Chapter 1 we discussed the concept of marginals, and we have used several different kinds of marginal analyses in the chapters that followed. A marginal analysis always takes a look at the effect of one more. So instead of going through the iterative process above to get the maximum profit, we can (and should) use marginals. Table 6.1 presents a hypothetical demand relationship that we can use to illustrate the first part of this concept.

Consistent with the demand relationship we have discussed so far, as price falls, quantity demanded increases. The third column, total revenue, is simply the product of price and quantity. In Table 6.2, we extend these data by adding a column showing marginal revenue.

As with all marginal concepts, marginal revenue tells us the effect of one more. In this case, marginal revenue tells us how much total revenue increases if we sell one more unit. For example, if we sell the third unit, total revenue increases from $88 (selling two units) to $117, so the marginal revenue of the third unit is $29. If we sell the fourth unit, revenue increases from $117 (three units) to $140, making the marginal revenue of the fourth unit $23.

TABLE 6.1
Demand and Total Revenue

Quantity	Price	Total Revenue
1	$50	$50
2	$44	$88
3	$39	$117
4	$35	$140
5	$33	$165

TABLE 6.2
Demand and Marginal Revenue

Quantity	Price	Total Revenue	Marginal Revenue
1	$50	$50	—
2	$44	$88	$38
3	$39	$117	$29
4	$35	$140	$23
5	$33	$165	$25

You may be wondering why the additional revenue we get from selling one more unit is not just the price. For example, if we go from selling three units to four units, the marginal revenue of the fourth unit is $23. Why isn't the price of the fourth unit $35? Because when we increase our sales from 3 to 4 units, we have to lower the price to do so. When we sell 3 units, we can charge a price of $39 per unit. If we want to sell another unit, we must lower our price to entice consumers to buy—that's the law of demand. When we lower the price, we do not just lower the price on the last (fourth) unit—we lower the price on all the units. Another way of looking at this is to think of the move from 3 to 4 units as having two parts: good news and bad news. The good news is that we are selling another unit, and we are getting $35 for it. The bad news is that we are now getting a lower price ($35) for the first 3 units than we were getting before ($39). That's a loss of $4 for each of those 3 units, or $12. Table 6.3 breaks this down.

TABLE 6.3
Effects of Lowering Price to Sell Another Unit

Gain	$35 on 4th unit
Loss	$12 ($4 each on units 1, 2, and 3 originally priced at $39 each and now priced at $35)
Net	$23 gain, or addition to total revenue

So, the marginal revenue of selling that fourth unit ($23) is less than the price we get ($35) because in order to sell the unit, we have to lower the price on the previous three units.

Once we know how much we will receive (net) from selling another unit, we can compare it to how much it costs to produce that unit. In other words, we will compare marginal revenue to marginal cost. Table 6.4 illustrates.

As the table shows, the total cost of producing one unit is $50, whereas the total cost of producing two units is $62. Therefore, the marginal cost of producing that second unit is $12. If we sell the second unit, we will get (net) $38 for it. If the addition to revenue is $38 and the cost to produce it is $12, should we do it? Of course—marginal revenue is greater than marginal cost. How about the third unit? If we sell that unit we will make $29, whereas the cost to make it was $19. Again, we should definitely do it. The marginal revenue of the fourth unit is $23—exactly equal to the cost of making it. You might think that it doesn't matter if we produce and sell this unit because we are getting only as much as it costs to make it. But we should keep producing and selling units up to and including the point at which marginal revenue is equal to marginal cost. Now look at the fifth unit. At this point, it costs $27 to make a unit, but the unit sells for only $25. We do not want costs to exceed benefits so we would not produce and sell this unit.

This brings us to the goal of all businesses: Regardless of what kind of competitive environment they find themselves in, they want to maximize profit. The way all firms achieve this is by producing and selling units to the point where marginal revenue is equal to marginal cost:

$$MR = MC$$

TABLE 6.4
Demand, Marginal Revenue, and Marginal Cost

Quantity	Price	Total Revenue	Marginal Revenue	Total Cost	Marginal Cost
1	$50	$50	—	$50	—
2	$44	$88	$38	$62	$12
3	$39	$117	$29	$89	$17
4	$35	$140	$23	$104	$23
5	$33	$165	$25	$131	$27

In our example, this firm maximizes profits at 4 units of output. Profit at this level of production is $36 ($140-$104). You can check the profit at the other levels of production—they all result in less profit than at 4 units.

Below we will look at firms' behavior in four different competitive environments. Each environment varies according to how many firms are in that market, the nature of the product they produce, and how they interact with each other. We will begin with perfect competition.

PERFECT COMPETITION

Perfect Competition	????	????	????

Description of Market

In a perfectly competitive environment, there are many buyers and sellers, and all firms are selling identical products. The combination of these two things means that no single participant in the market can change the product price. For example, if one firm decides that the market price is too low and tries to raise the price by withholding its product from the market (reducing supply), it will not be able to do so. There are many other firms selling the exact same product, so one producer pulling its product from the market will have no effect on the price. There are also no restrictions on producers entering or leaving this market. If a current producer wants to leave the market, it can do so fairly easily and at low cost. Conversely, if a firm that is currently not in this market wants to enter, it can do so easily and at low cost. This is called having no barriers to entry or exit.

In the real world, we find perfect competition in the stock market, commodities markets, and the markets for foreign exchange. In the market for gold, for example, an ounce of gold is just the same as any other ounce of gold—the products are all the same. Therefore, the market price for these goods cannot be manipulated by any single firm—it is set by the market as a whole.

Individual Firm Versus Market

Let's return to our market example from Chapter 2. The demand and supply schedules originally shown in Table 2.6 are presented again in Table 6.5.

The market equilibrium price and quantity are $0.75 and 6 units, respectively. Remember that we defined the market as many buyers and sellers coming together, so although we did not use the terminology at the time, we are really referring to a perfectly competitive market when referring to demand and supply relationships such as this.

The market price is $0.75, but what does this mean for an individual firm that is operating in this market? This firm is just one of many, many firms in the market, none of which can change the market price, regardless of how much or how little it produces. So each firm can produce any quantity it wants to and the

TABLE 6.5
Price and Quantity of Bubbly Pop

Price	Quantity Demanded	Quantity Supplied
$0.50	8	3
$0.75	6	6
$1.00	3	8
$1.25	1	10
$1.50	0	11

price it gets will be that market price—nothing more and nothing less. Table 6.6 shows the firm's demand schedule under these conditions.

Notice that for the market, the demand relationship is precisely as we discussed—in order for the *market* to sell another unit, the price must be lowered. This means that marginal revenue for the market will be less than the price. But the demand relationship for the *individual firm* is different. Demand for the firm's output can be any quantity, so the demand curve is horizontal at the market price.

The firm does not have to lower the price to sell another unit—it can sell all the units it wants to at whatever the market price is. If it tries to raise the price to $1.00, for example, it will find that it cannot sell any quantity because too

TABLE 6.6
Price and Quantity of Bubbly Pop: Individual Firm

Price	Quantity Demanded
$0.75	1
$0.75	2
$0.75	3
$0.75	4
$0.75	5
$0.75	6

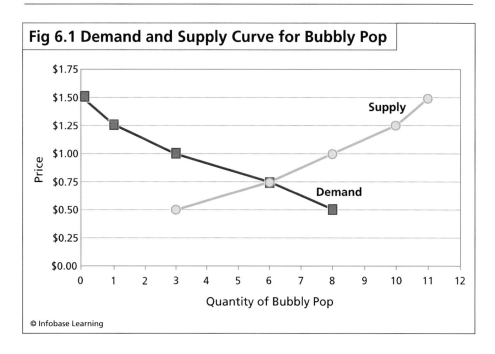

Fig 6.1 Demand and Supply Curve for Bubbly Pop

many other firms are in the market selling the identical product for $0.75. There is also no incentive for a firm to lower the price below $0.75 because it can sell all it wants to at that price. This means that for firms in a perfectly competitive

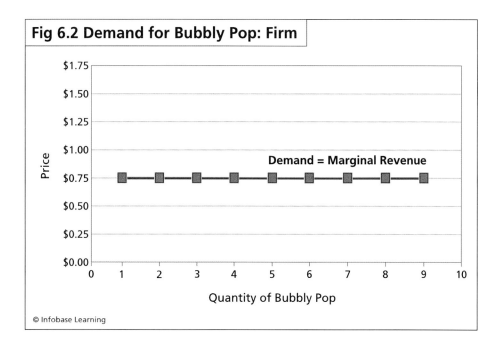

Fig 6.2 Demand for Bubbly Pop: Firm

TABLE 6.7

Price and Quantity of Bubbly Pop

Price	Quantity Demanded	Quantity Supplied
$0.50	12	3
$0.75	10	6
$1.00	8	8
$1.25	5	10
$1.50	3	11

environment, marginal revenue is the same thing as price. Each individual firm operating in a competitive environment accepts the market price as a factor beyond its control.

If market conditions change—for example, if there is an increase in demand—it is reflected in the market and individual demand schedules as shown in Table 6.7.

Table 6.8 shows what happens when the market experiences an increase in the equilibrium price—in this case to $1.00. That higher price is taken by each firm within the market as a given. From the firms' perspective it cannot be changed, just reacted to.

TABLE 6.8

Price and Quantity of Bubbly Pop: Individual Firm

Price	Quantity Demanded
$1.00	1
$1.00	2
$1.00	10
$1.00	20
$1.00	50
$1.00	1,000

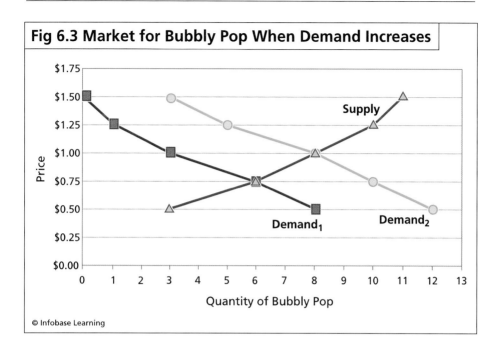

Fig 6.3 Market for Bubbly Pop When Demand Increases

The related graphs are presented in Figure 6.3 and Figure 6.4. When conditions in the market cause the equilibrium price to change, individual firms simply face a new price and demand curve.

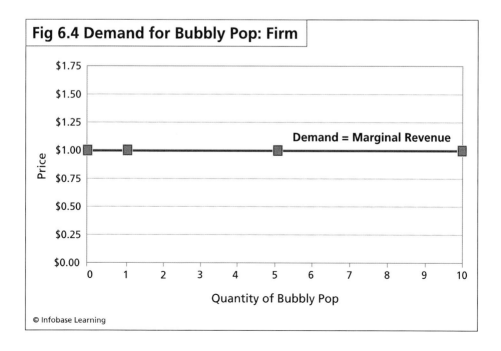

Fig 6.4 Demand for Bubbly Pop: Firm

If individual firms operating in an environment of perfect competition cannot change the price, what decision do they make? The primary decision made by these firms is a quantity decision. Given the market price, how much do they produce? We already know the answer to this question: They will produce until marginal revenue is equal to marginal cost. If we add costs to the firm's demand schedule, we could the results presented in Table 6.9.

This firm would get $0.75 if it sold the second unit of output, and it would cost $0.55 to produce this second unit. It is clear that the firm should produce and sell that unit. The third unit of output would net the firm $0.75 in revenue and cost $0.75 in costs to produce. Again, the firm should produce and sell this third unit. But look at the fourth unit. This unit would bring $0.75 in revenue to the firm, but producing it would cost $1.00. The firm would definitely not want to produce and sell this unit of output. This firm will maximize profit where marginal revenue is equal to marginal cost, at 3 units of output. Any fewer or any more units would lower profits.

But would the firm benefit from producing and selling 3 units? Not necessarily. Just because some level of output is the best the firm can do, does not mean producing that level of output is good business. If the profit-maximizing (or equivalently, the loss-minimizing) level of output does not provide a sufficient level of profit, the firm would not produce it. It would be better, in fact, to shut down and produce nothing. So let's examine whether 3 units of output is good enough. Let's add average total costs and look at the new breakdown in Table 6.10.

We already know that the best outcome this firm can produce is 3 units, where MR = MC. But is this "best" good enough? At 3 units of output, this firm is getting $0.75 per unit. At 3 units of output, this firm is incurring average total

TABLE 6.9
Individual Firm Marginal Revenue and Marginal Cost

Price = Marginal Revenue	Quantity Demanded	Total Cost	Marginal Cost
$0.75	1	$0.80	—
$0.75	2	$1.35	$0.55
$0.75	3	$2.05	$0.75
$0.75	4	$3.05	$1.00
$0.75	5	$4.32	$1.27
$0.75	6	$5.71	$1.39

TABLE 6.10
Individual Firm: Marginal Revenue and Costs

Price = Marginal Revenue	Quantity Demanded	Total Cost	Marginal Cost	Average Total Cost
$0.75	1	$0.80	—	$0.80
$0.75	2	$1.35	$0.55	$0.68
$0.75	3	$2.05	$0.75	$0.68
$0.75	4	$3.05	$1.00	$0.76
$0.75	5	$4.32	$1.27	$0.86
$0.75	6	$5.71	$1.39	$0.95

costs of $0.68 per unit. Recall from Chapter 5 that opportunity cost is already included in the cost figures. In other words, if the owner of the company had taken the money used to start the company and invested it in something else, it would have generated some level of return. We call this opportunity cost a **normal return,** and it is included in the cost figures. So costs include salaries, raw material, insurance, taxes, and a normal return. In this case, the firm is earning $0.75 per unit while the cost per unit is $0.68. Therefore, the firm is earning a profit that is greater than a normal return: an **economic profit** or an **above normal return.** This profit/return is sufficient to cover all explicit costs, plus the opportunity cost of owning the business (i.e., what the owner could have earned with that money by investing it elsewhere), plus more money on top of that. And if this one owner is making an economic profit, every firm in this industry is making an economic profit because all firms in a perfectly competitive industry are alike.

So what is likely to happen when a firm earns above normal returns? The first thing to consider is that entrepreneurs and investors are always looking for money-making opportunities, and our hypothetical industry is making above normal profits—money beyond what the next best use of funds would be. What will entrepreneurial people do? They will want to come into this industry so that they, too, can earn above normal profits.

Imagine for a moment that economic profit is a blinking, neon sign that says "Make Money Here." In the case of perfect competition, where the barriers to entry are low, firms are willing and able to respond to that signal and enter this money-making industry. But what happens when they do? Think back to the original demand and supply curves for the industry. How do these curves (and the market they represent) change if there are suddenly many more firms in this industry, all producing the same product? If you think supply would increase, you are right. If more firms are producing this product, then the supply of that product will increase. But remember what happens to price when supply increases—that is a shift of the supply curve to the right. Price falls and those above normal profits disappear. As long as above normal profits exist—that is, price is above average total cost—that signs blinks, and people respond by entering. The act of entering, however, causes price to fall.

How far will price fall? To answer this question we need to remember that price is falling because people outside the industry are entering the industry and increasing supply of the product. We also know this is happening because economic profits, which are higher than average total costs, is what is luring new firms into this industry. To work backwards, then, if price falls to a level equal to average total costs, then economic profits disappear, the "Make Money Here" signal stops blinking, and interest in entering this industry disappears because everyone in the industry is now making a normal return. The incentive to enter this industry has disappeared. Moreover, no one currently in the industry is unhappy because of this turn of events—everyone is making a normal return, covering their opportunity costs. Of course, they were a lot happier when they were making an above normal return, but in the case of perfect competition, those times are fleeting because of the lack of barriers to entry.

In perfect competition, many firms are selling identical products. Therefore, the only control a firm in this environment has is over the quantity it sells. Like all firms, the "best" quantity—the one that maximizes profits—is where MR = MC. The firm decides if this best quantity is good enough by comparing the price to average total cost for that level of production. If price is above average total costs, the firm will be very enthusiastic about producing and selling their output—they will be earning an economic profit. Unfortunately, the existence of an economic profit lights up that sign, encouraging others who are outside of the industry to enter in order to make money. Once others enter, however, price falls and will keep falling (others will keep entering) until the incentive to do so—economic profits—goes away. In a perfectly competitive environment in the long run, all firms are making a normal return. Any deviation from that is temporary as the incentive to enter disappears.

MONOPOLISTIC COMPETITION

Perfect Competition	Monopolistic Competition	????	????

The next stop on the continuum of market structures is **monopolistic competition**. Within the framework, we will present an industry that shares some of the characteristics of perfect competition but more closely represents many real-world firms.

Description of the Market

A market characterized by monopolistic competition has many firms, just like perfect competition. Also like perfect competition, this market has no barriers to entry, allowing other firms to enter if economic profits are being made. The big difference between the two types of markets is that in a monopolistic competitive market, the products are not identical. Sometimes there are actual physical differences in the products in this market. In other cases, the products are not really different, but consumers believe they are.

There are many examples of monopolistic competition, particularly in retailing where there are many types of shoe and clothing stores, for example. Other examples include companies that produce bleach, soap, aspirin, soup, and gasoline. Sometimes actual differences exist between these types of products, but in other cases, the products are really the same. Aspirin, for example, is a chemical compound, so the store brand of aspirin is physically the same as name-brand aspirin. To the extent that the name-brand companies can make consumers believe there is a difference (even when there is not), these firms enjoy a little bit of **market power**. This means that they do not have to accept the market price and simply react to it. They can, to some extent, control the price of their product by controlling the quantity that they produce. Remember that in perfect competition, a firm's choice of quantity has no effect on price. In monopolistic competition, firms face a demand curve that is downwardly sloping, just as we expect, so that decisions about quantity affect price. The demand curve has a negative slope (rather than being horizontal) because these firms' products are not identical. Whether the differences between the products are real or imagined, it gives firms some market power.

If product differentiation is the key in monopolistic competition, it stands to reason that advertising plays a very significant role in this industry. In perfectly competitive industries, advertising would be pointless—all the products are the same. But in monopolistically competitive industries, making consumers aware of (or creating) differences between products is what gives firms their ability to affect the price.

Because advertising represents a cost to the firm, the costs in monopolistically competitive industries are higher than in perfectly competitive ones. Higher costs mean higher prices. Although some economists look at these higher prices as a reflection of the waste associated with advertising (especially in the case of products that are really identical), it can also be seen as the price we pay for product diversity. For example, assume you need to buy some toothpaste. If the toothpaste industry were perfectly competitive, you would go into the story and find identical tubes on the shelf—each one exactly like every other one. But the fact is, you do not find identical tubes—you have a wide array of choices: paste or gel, whitening or not, spearmint or peppermint, and so forth. The prices for these diverse tubes are higher than they would be if all toothpastes were the same, but you also have choice—something you would not have with perfect competition.

Like perfect competition, monopolistically competitive industries have no barriers to entry, leading to similar outcomes. When firms in this industry are making above normal profits, an incentive exists for others outside of the industry to enter—the "Make Money Here" sign lights up. Given the lack of barriers, other firms can indeed enter. This time, however, the supply of the product does not increase because the products are not all identical. Because each one is slightly different from the others, we cannot look at the total supply because doing so would be like adding apples and oranges.

So what does happen when new firms enter this industry? From an individual firm's perspective, each new firm that enters, selling similar (but not identical) products, represents more competition—more possible substitutes for the original firm's product. If there are more substitutes available, demand for the original product will fall—shifting the demand curve to the left. Just as in perfect competition, new firms will stop entering this industry when the economic profits go away, and everyone in the industry is making a normal return.

To summarize these two market structures, both have many firms. Neither perfect competition nor monopolistic competition have barriers to entry, so if others outside the industry want to enter, they can. The difference between the two, however, is significant. In perfect competition, the products are identical, while in monopolistic competition, there is a difference (real or perceived) between the firms' products. The result of this difference is that firms in a monopolistically competitive industry can change the price with how much they produce. Because advertising is important in this industry, firms will not minimize their costs, leading to higher consumer prices than would be the case in a perfectly competitive market. In both cases, firms in the markets will earn a normal profit in the long run.

OLIGOPOLY

Perfect Competition	Monopolistic Competition	Oligopoly	????

The next stop on the continuum of market structures is **oligopoly**. In an oligopoly market, there are only a few firms—a sharp contrast to the many firms in perfect and monopolistic competition. Furthermore, these firms do not make decisions independently. Instead, they engage in interdependent decision-making—similar to a game of chess. One firm will try to anticipate what its rivals' reactions will be if it lowers the price of its product, for example, and create a strategy that is based on that anticipated response. In fact, this branch of economics is called **game theory.** This interdependence leads to many interesting situations, some of which will be presented later in this section.

There are many examples of oligopolistic industries: the automobile, airline, computer and gasoline industries to name a few. At this point it is important to differentiate between the producers of a product and the sellers of that product. A simple example illustrating this point involves the gasoline industry. You can buy gasoline almost anywhere; in some cases, you can find a gas station on every street corner—hardly the description of an oligopoly. But the retail outlet where you buy your gasoline is just that—an outlet that sells the product of a firm that produces that gasoline in an oligopolistic industry. Even though there are many places to buy gasoline, only a few firms refine it and provide it to the market.

Barriers to Entry

One of the other major differences between an oligopolistic industry and the two we previously discussed (perfect competition and monopolistic competition) relates to the issue of barriers to entry. In the former market structures, these barriers do not exist, In oligopolies, there are significant barriers preventing firms outside the industry from entering. These barriers are critical in how this market structure works.

Economies of Scale

Chapter 5 discussed economies of scale—when long run average cost falls as output increases. If a firm's economies of scale occur over a very small range of output, then it makes sense for many firms to be engaged in the industry in which this occurs. If just a few firms tried to provide the output for the entire market, they would be operating in the diseconomies of scale part of their average costs. On the other hand, if a firm's economies of scale extend over a wide range of output, it makes sense for only a few firms to provide the output for the market. For example, it would be very difficult for a brand new company to enter the airline industry because the capital investment is huge. A company can buy an airline, but a brand new firm starting an airline from scratch would have to buy a fleet of planes, establish routes, create a human resources department to recruit and hire pilots, baggage handlers, etc.—it would be a tremendous undertaking. A new firm just starting up would have much higher production costs than those of larger, established firms.

Government Barriers

Sometimes the government provides firms with barriers to entry to protect them from competition. Patents and copyrights, for example, give the firms that hold them exclusive rights of production for a period of time, protecting them from any and all other firms that would like to enter the industry. The govern-ment provides this barrier to encourage innovation—after all, no firm would invest large amounts of money into developing a new product if it could not also reap the reward for doing so. Once the patent expires (usually 14 years), the firm faces competition.

Control over an Input

Market power also comes from a firm's ability to control a vital input in the production process. For example, the mineral bauxite is a necessary input in the production of aluminum. If a company has control over bauxite mines, then it has effective control over the production of aluminum.

Oligopoly and Price

Whatever the nature of specific barriers to entry, the main result is that firms in oligopolistic industries have significant ability to affect the price. But price changes even within an oligopoly require thoughtful decisions and an understanding of potential consequences. When firms change their prices, for example, they do so knowing that their competitors within the industry may or may not change their price as well. Assume that an airline company is considering raising its airfares. Before doing so, they need to think about how their competitors will respond. On the one hand, their competitors may raise their airfares as well. If this occurs, everyone in the industry may earn more profit. On the other hand, their competitors may not raise their fares, seeing this decision as an opportunity to get customers away from the firm that raised its fares and earn even more profits. So whether to raise the price of airfares or not becomes a calculated risk—will everyone else follow suit, or will the company be left by itself, charging higher fares than everyone else? To understand how firms make these decisions, we need to look at some game theory basics.

The Prisoner's Dilemma

Two criminals, Bert and Ernie, have just been arrested by the police. They are charged with burglary, and the police have enough evidence for an open and shut case. However, the police also suspect that the two are responsible for a murder, but they do not have enough evidence to convict them of that crime—they need a confession from one of them. So they put Bert and Ernie in separate interview rooms and make each of them an offer. The evidence for the burglary is overwhelming, and if both suspects say nothing about the murder, they will each get 7 years in jail for the burglary. However, if one of them confesses to the murder, his sentence will be reduced to 3 years while the sentence for the other one (who did not confess) will be 30 years. If both of them confess, they each get 20 years. The police tell each one that whoever confesses first gets the best offer.

Fig 6.5 The Prisoner's Dilemma

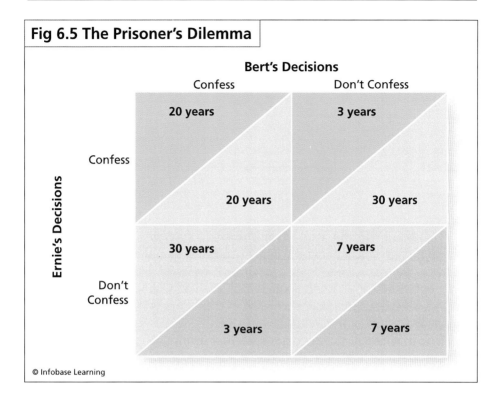

Bert's Decisions

	Confess	Don't Confess
Ernie's Decisions — Confess	20 years / 20 years	3 years / 30 years
Ernie's Decisions — Don't Confess	30 years / 3 years	7 years / 7 years

© Infobase Learning

Bert's and Ernie's choices are presented in Figure 6.5. Ernie's outcomes are in the upper diagonal and Bert's are in the lower diagonal.

What should each of them do? Clearly, the best outcome for them *jointly* is to remain quiet and not confess. This way, each of them gets 7 years for the burglary, but neither gets charged with the murder. Is this what will happen?

Let's look at Ernie's decision first. Ernie will try to do what is best for him, regardless of what Bert does. So Ernie thinks, "What if Bert confesses? What would be best for me?" The answer in this case is that Ernie should confess. If he does, he'll get 20 years, but if he does not (and Bert does), he'll get 30 years (look down the first column, for Bert confessing). But what if Bert does not confess? What's best for Ernie then? The same—he should confess (look down the second column, under Bert not confessing). If Ernie confesses, he will get 3 years; if he does not, he will get 7 years. So regardless of what Bert does (no matter which column—confess or don't confess), Ernie should confess.

Now let's look at Bert's decision. If he assumes that Ernie will confess, what's best for Bert is that he confesses (look at the first row, bottom diagonal). If Bert confesses (assuming Ernie does, too), he will get 20 years. If Bert does not confess, but Ernie does, Bert will get 30 years. If Bert thinks that Ernie will not confess (second row, lower diagonal), then, again, it is in his best interests to confess. If Ernie does not confess and Bert does, then Bert gets 3 years, but if Ernie does not confess and Bert does not, either, then Bert gets 7 years. Again, it is in Bert's best interests to confess, regardless of what Ernie does.

This situation is called the **prisoner's dilemma**. Even though both of them would be better off if neither confessed, that will not be the outcome. They will both confess, an outcome called the **dominant strategy**, even though that means each of them will spend 20 years in jail instead of 7 years. A decision maker's dominant strategy is what is best, regardless of what the other person or firm does.

But what if Bert and Ernie had discussed the possibility of getting caught and agreed that if that ever happened, they would both keep quiet? That means neither confesses, and they both get 7 years—that's a much better outcome than if they confess. Will this work? No, it won't. They each have an incentive to cheat on the agreement because if either confesses when the other does not, his sentence will be reduced to 3 years in jail. So even if they have an explicit agreement not to confess, they will because each of them will be made better off by doing so. The paradox is that when each of them does what is best for himself individually, it makes both of them worse off.

Firms in oligopolistic industries often find themselves in a similar position. Let's go back to the decision of whether to raise airfares or not. We will assume that there are only two airlines in this industry, In the Clouds Airlines and Flying High Airlines, and each of them has two choices: to charge a low price or a high price. Their profits will be higher if they charge a high price, but they have to consider that the other airline might undercut their price to attract customers. Figure 6.6 breaks down their decision options.

The upper diagonal shows In the Clouds' outcomes (profits, in this case), and the lower diagonals show those for Flying High. If they both charge a low price, their profits are $3 million each. If they both charge a high price, they each earn $5 million in profit. Clearly, it is in both of their interests to charge a high price because that means both earn a higher profit. But if In the Clouds charges a low price whereas Flying High charges a high price, In the Clouds will make more profit because it will attract customers away from Flying High—In the Clouds will make $7 million and Flying High will only make $1 million. Likewise, if Flying High charges a low fare and In the Clouds charges a high fare, Flying High will earn $7 million in profit and In the Clouds will only make $1 million.

Let's look at the dominant strategy for each company. From the perspective of In the Clouds, if Flying High charges a low price (looking down the first column), the best decision is to charge a low price. In the Clouds can earn $3 million by charging a low price or $1 million by charging a high price. On the other hand, if Flying High charges a high price (looking down the second column), In the Clouds would still choose to charge a low price ($7 million compared

Fig 6.6 The Prisoner's Dilemma and Business Strategy

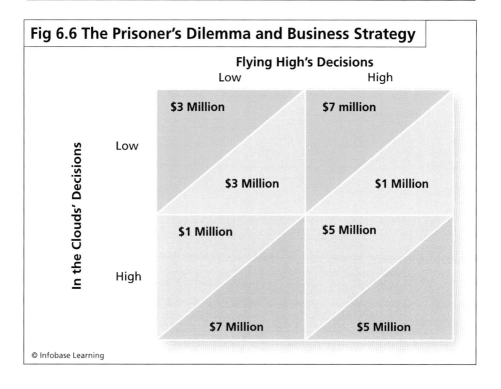

© Infobase Learning

to $5 million). Now let's change the perspective and look at things from the standpoint of Flying High (looking across rows). If In the Clouds charges a low price, Flying High will compare profits of $3 million (low price) and $1 million (high price) and choose to charge a low price. Likewise, if In the Clouds charges a high price, Flying High will choose the low price ($7 million compared to $5 million). Therefore, even though they would both be better off if they charged a high price (thus earning profits of $5 million each), they will both charge a low price—that is their dominant strategy.

Now consider what would happen if the two companies got together and agreed to charge a high price? There are two things wrong with this strategy. To begin with, this kind of arrangement is called **collusion**. The term refers to any attempt by firms to get together to explicitly control price or quantity, and this is illegal in the United States. Secondly, even if there were no laws preventing them from agreeing on the high price, this agreement would not last. If one of them is charging a high price, it is in the best interests of the other one to charge a low price and entice customers away, increasing profits. But if one of them offers a low price, the other one has to as well to keep from losing customers, and the whole agreement falls apart. As in the case of Bert and Ernie, both firms have an incentive to cheat on the agreement that would have made both better off.

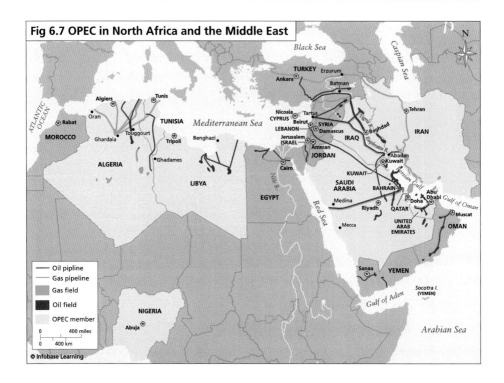

Fig 6.7 OPEC in North Africa and the Middle East

Although explicit agreements like this are illegal in the United States, they are permitted in other parts of the world. One of the best examples of a collusive agreement is OPEC (Organization of Petroleum Exporting Countries). OPEC is a **cartel** that controls virtually all of the oil supply in the Middle East by assigning production quotas to its member countries. If each country produces the amount of oil OPEC has told it to produce, the quantity supplied is kept at a low enough level to keep price high. According to what we have seen above, the parties to the agreement should have an incentive to cheat, resulting in the disintegration of the agreement. Despite this, OPEC has survived for years. The obvious question here is "why?" There is certainly an incentive for member countries to cheat—if the price of oil is high, it is tempting for a member country to produce more than it is supposed to and gain large profits at that high price. But member countries do not cheat because there is an enforcement mechanism. If a country cheats and produces more than its quota, it faces strong sanctions from the organization. An enforcement mechanism achieves what the countries, acting individually, could not—it allows member countries to operate in a way that is best for all of them collectively.

Firms in oligopolistic industries make strategic decisions about issues other than just price. Sometimes that decision means doing nothing. In 1970 Congress passed legislation prohibiting cigarette advertising on television and radio. None of the cigarette producers appeared during hearings to oppose the legislation. Why not? Wouldn't you expect that the cigarette producers would vehemently oppose this ban? Let's find out why they did not by looking at this situation within the framework of the prisoner's dilemma.

Advertising on television and radio costs cigarette manufacturers a lot of money. All firms in this industry would benefit if they did not buy these expensive ads, but no single firm could not stop advertising because doing so would have put it at a disadvantage if competitors continued to advertise. In other words, collectively, all of the firms would be better off if none of them advertised, saving them all a lot of money. But even if they all agreed not to advertise, each firm would have an incentive to cheat on that agreement, advertising when its competitors did not. Soon, everyone would have to start advertising again and the agreement would unravel. But, if there were some way of enforcing the no-advertising position, all of these companies would benefit. In this case, the government took on the role of enforcer. Just like the enforcement role of OPEC has ensured that member countries operate in their collective best interests, the U.S. government's ban on cigarette advertising ensures that cigarette companies will not advertise. Cigarette companies refrained from opposing the government's decision because allowing that decision to become law was in their collective best interests.

Firms in oligopolistic industries earn profits that are greater than a normal return. These high economic profits make other firms want to come into these industries, just as with perfect competition and monopolistic competition. The difference here is that because of barriers to entry, new firms cannot join these industries. Therefore, in oligopolistic industries, above normal profits can continue in the long run.

MONOPOLY

Perfect Competition	Monopolistic Competition	Oligopoly	Monopoly

The last type of market structure examined in this chapter is monopoly, a structure that lies at the opposite end of the continuum from perfect competition. A **monopoly** is characterized by only one firm, so the firm and the industry are the same thing. A monopoly has significant barriers to entry, just as oligopolistic firms do. These barriers allow monopolists to earn economic profits in the long run, preventing new firms from entering. A monopoly typically produces a good or service for which there are no close substitutes. If a substitute were readily available, the monopoly would not really be a monopoly. Examples of this market structure are utility companies, cable companies, and a drug company that holds a patent for a new medicine.

A common misperception about monopolies is that they can charge any price they want to charge and sell any quantity they want to sell. This is not true.

Even though a monopoly is the only firm selling a particular product, it cannot force consumers to buy it. A monopoly is still constrained by the demand curve, meaning that as it raises its price, consumers will want less. But what about utility companies? In most states, utilities are controlled by monopolies. It is true that we cannot decide to switch to another utility company if the rates get too high. But we can change the thermostat, weatherproof our houses, turn off lights when we leave a room. In other words, even though we cannot take our business elsewhere, we can and do respond to price increases by lowering quantity—just like the demand relationship says we will. A monopoly can decide on the price, and consumers will respond with a quantity; or the monopoly can set the quantity, and the market will determine what the price will be. In other words, the monopoly sets either price or quantity, and the market determines the other.

Maximizing Profit

How do monopolies maximize profit? We already know that any firm sets MR = MC to maximize profit. For a perfect competitor, marginal revenue and price are identical because the firm has no ability to control the price. A monopoly can control the price, but if it wants to sell another unit, it must lower the price. Otherwise, consumers will not buy the extra quantity. Let's look at a hypothetical monopolistic market for jeans. Table 6.11 provides a breakdown of components you are already familiar with: quantity, price, total revenue, marginal revenue, and marginal cost.

TABLE 6.11
Monopoly Market for Jeans

Quantity	Price	Total Revenue	Marginal Revenue	Marginal Cost
1	$95	$95	—	—
2	$90	$180	$85	$40
3	$85	$255	$75	$45
4	$80	$320	$65	$50
5	$75	$375	$55	$55
6	$70	$420	$45	$60
7	$65	$455	$35	$65
8	$60	$480	$25	$70

In a monopoly, the firm *is* the industry, so the market demand curve for jeans will be the same as the individual firm's demand curve. If this firm wants to increase its sale of jeans from one pair to two pairs, it needs to lower its price from $95 to $90. We get total revenue by multiplying price by quantity. Our marginal revenue is how much total revenue increases if we sell one more unit, and marginal cost is given. Like all firms in all types of industries, a monopoly will maximize profit at the point where marginal revenue is equal to marginal cost. The marginal revenue of the fourth unit, for example, is $65, while the marginal cost of producing that unit is $50. Therefore, this unit should be produced and sold. But at 5 units, marginal revenue is equal to marginal cost and that level of production maximizes profit for the firm. At 6 units, marginal revenue is $45 while marginal cost is $60—this unit should be not be produced and sold because the firm would lose money on that unit.

Monopoly Versus Perfect Competition

As noted at the beginning of this section, monopoly and perfect competition are at opposite ends of our market structure continuum. One has many firms, all selling the same product; the other has only one firm selling a product that does not have any close substitutes. A perfect competitor has no market power and makes normal profits in the long run. A monopoly has a lot of market power and can continue to enjoy economic profits in the long run because of barriers to entry. They also differ on their choice of profit maximizing quantities. Let's take another look at Table 6.11.

The monopoly chooses to produce and sell 5 pairs of jeans because that represents the point where marginal revenue is equal to marginal cost. It can sell these 5 pairs of jeans for $75 each. But what if these were the data for a perfectly competitive market? In perfect competition, profit maximization also occurs (like all firms) where marginal revenue is equal to marginal cost. The difference with perfect competitors is that marginal revenue and demand (market price) are the same thing. If we look at the table, we see that price is equal to marginal cost at 7 units of output. At this level of output, the perfect competitor's price would be $65 for a pair of jeans. So, a monopoly would produce 5 pairs of jeans and charge $75 a pair, whereas a perfectly competitive industry would produce 7 pairs of jeans and charge $65 a pair. The bottom line here is that a monopoly does not produce as much output and charges a higher price compared to a perfectly competitive firm.

Is a Monopoly "Bad"?

From the perspective of consumers, it is easy to understand why a monopoly may not get voted the most popular market structure. After all, as the jeans market example in the previous section illustrated, a monopoly does not provide as much output to the market and charges a higher price, relative to a perfectly competitive firm. Furthermore, monopolies are big, have a lot of market power, and can earn economic profits—for a long time. So what's to like? Well, maybe not a lot, but they do have some redeeming qualities.

One of these relates to economies of scale. We discussed this in relation to barriers to entry. If one firm—the monopoly—can produce a large amount of output and still be enjoying economies of scale, then it should do so. The alternative is that more than one firm produces this output, each producing a smaller quantity than a single monopoly would. But a smaller quantity means a higher cost per unit, so costs could rise for consumers if more than one firm produced in this market. This might seem to contradict our result above, that monopolists charge a higher price than a perfect competitor. It does—this is a very special case of monopoly, and there is no guarantee that the monopoly would pass along its lower production costs to consumers in the form of lower prices.

The other redeeming feature of monopolies is that they consistently earn above normal profits. Although this might not seem to be a good thing for consumers, it can be. Monopolies can invest in research and development, eventually bringing new products to the market that firms in a more competitive environment cannot do. Suppose, for example, that a major drug company is granted a patent on a new medicine for diabetes. The patent, in essence, grants this company a monopoly on the new medicine once it is produced. There is a very good reason for this. Producing a new medicine generally requires a significant investment of time and money for research and development. If this company does not have the assurance that it will be granted the patent (thus giving it a monopoly), it would have no incentive to invest millions of dollars in creating the drug in the first place. If other firms were allowed to duplicate the drug as soon as it was released into the market, the monopoly would have no opportunity to recoup its investment. Research and development in monopolistic markets can lead to advances in certain areas that are prohibitively expensive for firms in other market structures. But these activities are likely to occur more readily and more frequently when a monopoly's investments are protected from competition.

SUMMARY

Firms operate in a variety of competitive environments, ranging from many firms to only one firm. The particular kind of environment determines whether a firm has any market power, whether it will engage in advertising, whether its profits will continue in the long run, and a host of other factors. But all firms have a common objective: maximizing profit. And in each case, this objective is reached when marginal revenue is equal to marginal cost.

Further Reading

Levitt, S.J., and S.J. Dubner. *Freakonomics: A Rogue Economist Explains the Hidden Side of Everything.* New York: HarperCollins, 2005.

———. *Superfreakonomics: Global Cooling, Patriotic Prostitutes, and Why Suicide Bombers Should Buy Life Insurance.* New York: HarperCollins, 2009.

Milgrom, P., and J. Roberts. *Economics, Organization, and Management.* New York: Prentice Hall, 1992.

Poundstone, W. *Prisoner's Dilemma.* New York: Doubleday, 1992.

Rosenthal, E.C. *The Complete Idiot's Guide to Game Theory.* New York: Penguin Group, 2011.

## CHAPTER 7

THE LABOR MARKET

INTRODUCTION
In some ways the market for labor is very similar to the market structures and individual market components previously discussed. The market for labor is reflected by demand and supply curves, for example, and external factors cause these curves to shift. But in other, very important ways, the market for labor is very different. After all, this is a market for people, not inanimate objects, and that creates special circumstances that we will examine in this chapter. Looking at the labor market provides answers to some new and interesting questions about microeconomics, such as why tickets to professional sporting events are so expensive. Think you know the answer?

THE LABOR MARKET: OVERVIEW
In our discussions of other markets, the participants have been clearly defined. Those on the demand side of the market are individuals—consumers. Those on the supply side of the market are firms—those who produce. When we talk about the labor market, those roles are reversed. In this market firms are the ones who demand labor, and individuals are the ones who supply it.

Another way in which labor markets are different from other markets is that those who demand labor (firms) have a specific motivation that is very different from typical consumer motivation. Those who demand anything else—pizza, shoes, or haircuts—all want goods or services for the pleasure or usefulness these things provide as they are being consumed. Firms, on the other hand, do not demand labor because they like having a bunch of people hanging around the business all day. They demand labor because labor helps them produce their products. In other words, their demand for labor is entirely dependent upon the demand for their product—it is a **derived demand**. If the demand for a firm's product is high, the demand for labor will be high. If the demand for the product is low, the demand for labor will also be low. This demand is derived, or flows from, the demand for the final output.

THE DEMAND FOR LABOR

Before addressing demand for labor, it's a good idea to review some aspects of production, and we can do this by revisiting our shirt-making enterprise introduced in Chapter 5. The most important thing to keep in mind during this review is that firms do not demand labor just to have people around. They demand labor because of the output that labor can produce.

In this example, when one worker is hired, he or she can produce 4 shirts. When two workers are hired, they can produce a total of 9 shirts. Because output goes up by 5 shirts with the hiring of the second worker, this worker's marginal product is 5. Marginal product reaches its maximum value (7) with the hiring of 3 workers. Should this firm hire more than 3 workers if marginal product decreases after the third worker is hired? There are two pieces of information

TABLE 7.1
Workers and Number of Shirts Produced

# of Workers (L)	# of Shirts Produced (Q)	Marginal Product (MP)
0	0	—
1	4	4
2	9	5
3	16	7
4	22	6
5	26	4
6	28	2
7	28	0
8	25	−3

that this firm needs to consider before answering this question and the bigger question about the optimal level of hiring. One thing to be considered here is how much each unit of output can be sold for. The other is how much it would cost to get each additional worker—the wage rate.

Let's look at the first piece of information—the price of the output. Assume that this firm can sell each unit of output for $2. Table 7.2 includes a column that reflects this new information, which is called marginal revenue product.

Marginal revenue product is found by multiplying marginal product by marginal revenue. Remember that in perfect competition marginal revenue and price are the same thing, so each entry in the marginal product column is simply multiplied by $2. That's how we *compute* marginal revenue product; now we'll look at what this means. If this firm hires the second worker, that worker will add 5 units to how much the firm produces. If each of those units sells for $2, the second worker is producing $10 of value for the firm, meaning this worker is "worth" $10 to the firm. The third worker produces $14 of value for the firm, the fourth worker, $12, and so on.

In order to maximize profit, this firm needs to compare how much value each worker produces to how much it costs to get this worker. Let's assume

TABLE 7.2

Number of Workers and Marginal Revenue Product

# of Workers (L)	# of Shirts Produced (Q)	Marginal Product (MP)	Marginal Revenue Product (MRP: P = $2)
0	0	—	—
1	4	4	$8
2	9	5	$10
3	16	7	$14
4	22	6	$12
5	26	4	$8
6	28	2	$4
7	28	0	$0
8	25	−3	−$6

that the wage rate is $10. Should the firm hire the first worker? Because the value of this worker to the firm is $8 and it would cost $10 to get this worker, it seems reasonable to conclude that the firm should not hire this first worker. But that would be incorrect. For one thing, if there were no first worker, there would be no shirts. But beyond this obvious reason is another important reason: Up until the point of diminishing returns—where marginal product reaches a maximum—total output increases at an increasing rate. That is, every time a worker is hired, total output not only increases, but it increases by more than the increase contributed by the previous worker.

The reason for this is that workers become more productive when they can specialize. So, instead of one worker doing everything, two workers can divide the work, with the first performing one task while the second performs another task. Gains in production from specialization can extend over several workers, depending on what they are producing and how the production process is set up. Regardless of how many workers it has, a firm would never want to stop hiring workers when it is still in this range (i.e., up until the point of diminishing returns—where marginal product reaches a maximum) because each additional worker not only increases output, but increases it more than the person before! A firm can benefit only if it keeps hiring additional workers all through this range because the more workers that are hired, the more productive the workforce is.

So let's get back to how many workers should be hired in our shirt manufacturing company. The first worker produces value to the firm worth $8, but it costs $10 to hire this person. Should the firm do this? Yes, because the firm will gain from specialization as it hires more workers, until the point of diminishing returns. The second worker produces value of $10 to the firm, and it costs $10 to get this worker. Should this worker be hired? Yes, again—because the firm is still benefiting from specialization. The third worker produces value of $14

TABLE 7.3
Wage and Number of Workers Demanded

Wage	Number of Workers
$7	5
$10	4
$13	3

to the firm, and hiring this person means the same $10 cost as with the others. This worker, too, should be hired, as should the fourth worker ($12 gain compared to $10 cost).

Now what about the fifth worker? This worker generates $8 to the firm while costing the firm $10. This worker should not be hired. Unlike the first worker (who also produced output valued at $8), this worker generates less output than the worker before (worker 4), so the firm has realized all its benefit from specialization (marginal product is declining). From this point, no additional workers should be hired.

You may recognize that this analysis is just a special case of the profit maximizing condition in the output market—firms should produce where marginal revenue is equal to marginal cost. In the case of labor, the marginal revenue (or, more broadly, marginal benefit) is the value of the last worker, and marginal cost is the wage. So, in this case, the number of workers the firm should hire to maximize profit is four.

What if the wage rate fell to $7—how many workers should the firm hire? You should be able to see that the firm should hire five workers. The fifth worker generates a value of $8, which is greater than the wage. The sixth worker, however, is worth only $4 to the firm and should not be hired, even at a wage of $7. If the wage increased to $13, the firm should hire only three workers. Let's put these combinations of wages and number of workers in a table (Table 7.3).

So as the wage (the price of labor) increases, the firm wants to hire fewer workers. Does this sound like a familiar relationship? It should—it's a demand relationship. And because we got the number of workers in this table from the MRP column in the Table 7.2, we can think of MRP and the demand for labor as being the same thing.

If we graph the first and last columns of Table 7.2 (number of workers and MRP), we get the results shown in Figure 7.1. Just as we saw in the table, marginal product starts to fall after the third worker is hired, indicating that the firm has realized all the gains to be had from specialization.

Figure 7.2 shows what happens when we add the various wage rates. When the wage rate is $13 (blue line), the wage line intersects the MRP function between 3 and 4 workers. We know that the firm would not hire 4 workers when wage is $13 because the fourth worker provides less value to the firm than $13 (and you can't hire a fraction of a worker), so it would stop at 3 workers. When the wage is $10 (green line), it intersects the MRP function at four workers (rounding down) and at 5 workers when the wage is $7 (purple). We can see that the MRP curve serves the same function as a demand curve—it relates price with quantity. In this case, the price is the wage, and the quantity is the number of workers.

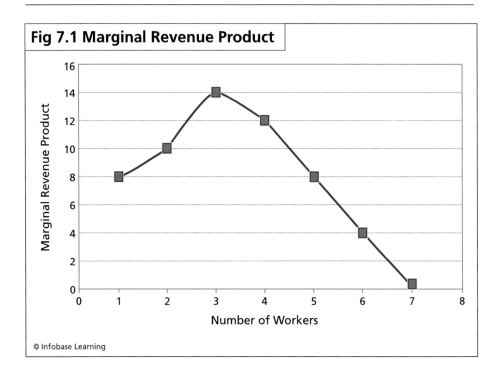

Fig 7.1 Marginal Revenue Product

© Infobase Learning

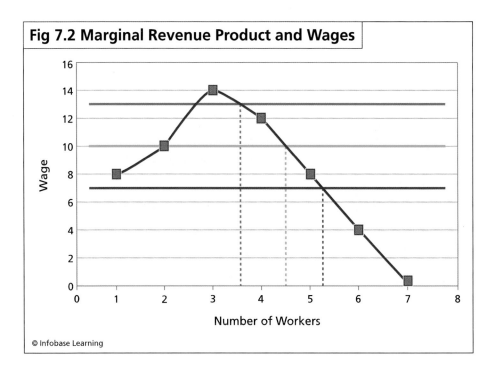

Fig 7.2 Marginal Revenue Product and Wages

© Infobase Learning

SHIFTS IN THE DEMAND FOR LABOR

Just as the demand curve for a product shifts when factors other than its price change, the demand curve for labor shifts when factors other than the wage change. Four additional factors that can cause this shift are explained below.

Price of the Output

If marginal revenue product is the same thing as demand for labor, it makes sense that when the components of marginal revenue product change, so will demand. Specifically, what if the firm can get more for its output? In our previous example, we assumed that the price of each unit of output was $2. But what if the demand for the firm's product increases, and it can now get $3 per unit? What happens to the demand for labor?

Because we get the marginal revenue product by multiplying marginal revenue (price) times marginal product, it follows that if price increases, so will MRP. Each individual worker is producing the same amount as before, but suddenly each worker is more valuable to the firm than before because

TABLE 7.4

Number of Workers and Marginal
Revenue Product with Change in Output Price

# of Workers (L)	# of Shirts Produced (Q)	Marginal Product (MP)	Marginal Revenue Product (MRP: P = $3)
0	0	—	—
1	4	4	$12
2	9	5	$15
3	16	7	$21
4	22	6	$18
5	26	4	$12
6	28	2	$6
7	28	0	$0
8	25	-3	-$9

each worker's output is worth more. The demand curve shifts to the right (Figure 7.3).

For any given wage, firms will now want to hire more workers than before because each worker is more valuable to them. If the output price were to decrease, each worker would be producing something of less value to the firm, so the firm would demand fewer workers as the demand curve shifts to the left.

It is important to recognize at this point that the wage is not causing demand changes. Back in Chapter 2, we differentiated between a movement along the demand curve and a shift of the curve. When a good's price changes, that change causes a movement along the demand curve. But we later discovered that these price changes are caused by supply curve shifts. So a shift in the supply curve causes movements along a demand curve. When another factor changes, the demand curve shifts, causing a change in the price. It works the same way here—the wage is *determined* by shifts in the demand curve—a change in the wage does not *cause* a demand curve to shift.

Worker Productivity
What happens to the demand for labor if the workers became more productive? Perhaps they have gone through training, or new technology allows them to produce more per hour. Whatever the reason, the demand for workers will go up because marginal product (which will increase as workers increase productivity) is a component of marginal revenue product.

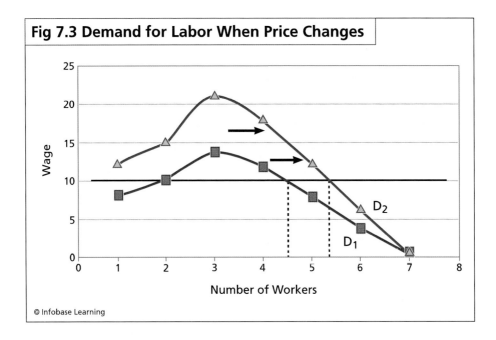

Fig 7.3 Demand for Labor When Price Changes

TABLE 7.5
Demand for Labor When Productivity Increases

# of Workers (L)	# of Shirts Produced (Q)	Marginal Product (MP)	Marginal Revenue Product (MRP: P = $2)
0	0	—	—
1	6	6	$12
2	14	8	$16
3	24	10	$20
4	31	7	$14
5	36	5	$10
6	40	4	$8
7	40	0	$0
8	39	−1	−$2

The output is still selling for $2 each, but each worker is more valuable to the firm because he or she is producing more units than before. Again, the demand curve will shift to the right, just as with an increase in output price.

Technological Changes
Technological changes were mentioned in the previous section, but because of its effect on the demand for labor, we should look more closely at this factor. Sometimes firms will adopt a new technology that increases workers' productivity. When word processing programs replaced typewriters, for example, the productivity of secretarial workers increased. When technology makes labor more productive, the demand curve for labor shifts to the right, increasing the demand for labor. But the role of technology is not always to complement worker productivity. Sometimes technology substitutes for labor. Assembly line workers have increasingly been replaced by robots, for example. In this case, when technology substitutes for labor, a firm will demand less labor as the demand curve shifts left.

Number of Firms
When new firms start up, the demand for labor will increase, and the demand curve will shift to the right. If firms go out of business, the curve will shift to the left and fewer workers will be demanded.

SUPPLY OF LABOR

Just as the market for a good or service as two sides, so does the market for labor. Individuals are the suppliers of labor to firms, deciding how much labor to offer to the market. We will assume that when individuals provide their labor, their opportunity cost (what they are giving up) is time that could be spent engaged in leisure. Of course, it works the other way, too—the opportunity cost of leisure is the wage you could have earned instead. Therefore, the higher the wage, the greater the opportunity cost of leisure. Just as with everything else, the more expensive something becomes, the less of it you want. So as the wage increases, leisure becomes more expensive (the opportunity cost is higher). So you consume less leisure and work more.

This gives us the familiar, positive relationship between price and quantity for supply curves—but in this case, price is the wage and quantity is the number of workers. There is a minimum wage that individuals will accept to be pulled into the labor market. This is called the **reservation wage**. You can imagine that if you were offered a job for $0.25 an hour, you probably would not take it—it is below your minimally acceptable wage—your reservation wage. What about $1.00 an hour? You may not accept that wage, but there are others who would, so they will be pulled into the labor market. What about $5.00 an hour? Again, this might be unacceptable to you but

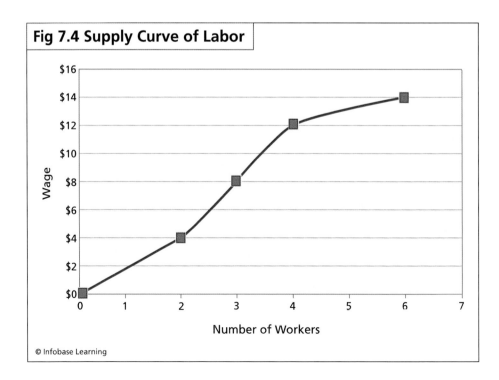

Fig 7.4 Supply Curve of Labor

© Infobase Learning

acceptable to others, and these others would also be pulled into the labor market. Eventually, the wage will be high enough to cover your reservation wage, so you would be willing to give up your leisure and work. Again, this describes a positive relationship between wages and number of workers supplied to the labor market—the greater the wage, the greater the number of people entering the market.

SHIFTS OF THE SUPPLY CURVE
Just as with demand, several factors can shift the supply curve. As you read about these factors, remember that increases in supply are represented by a shift to the right, while decreases in supply are shown by a shift of the curve to the left.

Changes in Population
It may seem obvious that increases in population result in an increase in the supply of labor, but it is a bit more complicated than that. For example, to the extent that immigrants are employed in lower-skilled occupations, a relaxation of immigration laws leads to an increase in the population of these workers, reducing the wage in some occupations that are heavy users of low-skilled workers.

Changes in Demographics
Changes in demographics are related to changes in population, but just certain segments of it. Two real-life demographic changes easily illustrate this point. In the 1970s, women began entering the labor market in large numbers, and the labor supply increased, shifting the curve to the right. A more current example involves the baby boomers (a large segment of the population of the United States today). As baby boomers retire and leave the labor force, the labor supply curve will shift back to the left, decreasing supply.

Changes in Choices
At the heart of the labor supply curve is opportunity cost—what you are giving up when you work in a particular labor market. As noted above, one opportunity cost of working is giving up leisure, but accepting work in one labor market also means you are giving up work in all other labor markets. Let's assume for example that you are working as a nurse. You notice that the wage for emergency medical technicians (the people who staff ambulances) is very high. This is a similar field to yours, with similar requirements, so you shift from the nursing labor market to the EMT labor market. Presumably, other nurses will do the same thing. The result is that the labor supply in the nursing market will decrease (the curve will shift to the left), and the labor supply in the EMT market will increase (the curve will shift to the right).

EQUILIBRIUM IN THE LABOR MARKET

Labor markets work the same way as the market for anything else, including the equilibrium that results from bringing both sides of the market together. So when we bring demand and supply together, we achieve an equilibrium wage and number of workers. In the shirt manufacturing example we've been using throughout this volume, when the price of the output is $2, equilibrium means 4 workers and a market-clearing wage of $12. But as we have seen at various points along the way, things rarely stay the same. What happens when the demand for labor changes? Let's assume that the demand for the firm's output increases. As we know, the demand curve will shift to the right. Now we see that this pushes up the wage of the workers in this labor market, as well as the number of workers employed.

Chapter 2 explained several things that can happen in the market for a product when its supply increases. The same things can occur in the labor market. We'll revisit the example of significant wage differences between nurses and EMTs to illustrate. As previously noted, nurses in this example have an incentive to leave nursing and become EMTs because the wage in that market is higher than what can make in nursing. Responding to this, many nurses leave nursing and become EMTs. As a result, labor supply in the nursing field declines, while labor supply in the EMT market grows.

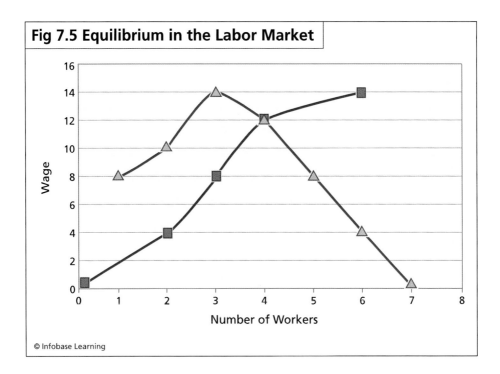

Fig 7.5 Equilibrium in the Labor Market

© Infobase Learning

Fig 7.6 Changes in the Labor Market

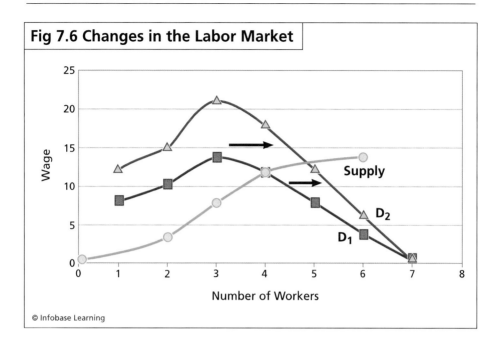

© Infobase Learning

Now let's think about what that does to wages in both markets. As nurses leave that market and supply decreases, the wage for nurses will increase. As they enter the EMT market and supply increases, wages in that market will be pushed down. The irony is that the reason that nurses left the nursing labor market and entered the EMT labor market was because the wages in the former were lower compared to wages in the latter. But by acting on this incentive and moving into the EMT labor market, they will actually force the wage down in their new market, and conversely, force the wage up in their old market.

WAGES: WHO GETS WHAT AND WHY
You already know how wages are determined within a particular labor market: Demand and supply factors come together in a market and establish wages and employment levels. But why do wages differ *between* labor markets? And what makes them differ so much?

Human Capital Requirements
One of the main reasons that different jobs pay different wages is that the amount of **human capital** required to do them differs. Human capital is the investment people make in themselves—education, training, even preventive health. Just as with other kinds of investment, people invest in human capital because they expect a payoff at the end of the investment period. When you make the decision to attend college, you are making a human capital investment decision—one you make because you expect your salary potential to be

The Price of a Ticket

Let's look back at our question posed at the beginning of the chapter: why are tickets to professional sporting events so expensive? Most people think the tickets are expensive because team owners have to make prices high enough to cover player salaries. Actually the causation runs the opposite direction: Player salaries are high because ticket prices are high!

Think of the price of tickets as the price of the output for a manufacturing firm. Just like with a firm's output, the price of tickets is determined by the market. If lots of people like and want Bubbly Pop, the demand for Bubbly Pop goes up and so does the price. Ticket prices are determined by fan demand—the more people want to see a game, the higher the price of tickets. In each case, the price is driven up by an increase in demand.

We already know what happens when the price of the firm's output increases—it causes the demand for labor to shift, driving up the price of labor, in this case the player salaries. So the general wisdom that player salaries cause high ticket prices is not just a little inaccurate—it's exactly backwards!

Yankee stadium. The New York Yankees have the highest payroll of any American sports team as well as the most expensive ticket prices in Major League Baseball. An increase in demand drives up the price of sporting event tickets, leading to a rise in player salaries. *(Wikipedia. Matt Boulton)*

greater when you finish college than if you had stopped at a high school degree. Jobs that require a lot of human capital generally pay higher wages than those with lower human capital requirements. Otherwise, there would be no incentive for people to acquire the human capital necessary to get those jobs. For example, it takes a lot of human capital accumulation to become a medical doctor. The wage for doctors is generally very much higher than the median wage, but it should be. If it were not, no one would have the incentive to go through all the schooling necessary to become a doctor.

But given this explanation about human capital, how do you explain someone like Peyton Manning? In 2010, Peyton Manning was the highest paid NFL player, earning two, three, and more times what some other NFL players make. Peyton Manning has exceptional talent —but is he three times (or more) better than any other player? Probably not, but this extreme wage differential does not always come about because people are three or ten or even hundred times better than others in their field. The real reason is that some labor markets have "superstars" who command a much higher salary than their peers do. This often applies to professional athletes or actors and actresses with box office appeal, although it can also apply to people in other professions (e.g., medicine or technology). These individuals may be better, but not *that* much better than others in their respective fields. What drives superstar salaries is demand for a particular person. For example, many people attended NFL games just to watch Manning play. This increases the demand for tickets, increasing his marginal revenue product, which means his wage goes up. The wage differential between superstars and others in the same field is much greater than the human capital or ability differential between them.

Compensating Wage Differentials

One reason that labor markets have different wages is that some jobs are more attractive than others. Garbage collectors, fire fighters, oil rig workers, sewer workers, all may be paid a higher wage than workers who work in safer, cleaner surroundings; the higher wages compensate them for hazardous or unpleasant working conditions. But compensating wage differentials sometimes work the other way as well. If someone works in a job that offers flexible hours, the opportunity to travel a lot on the company's dime, and similar amenities, it is likely that the wages may not be as high as those paid in jobs without such amenities.

Unions and Professional Organizations

Some workers are covered by union contracts, which can raise wages above what they otherwise would be. Unions are organizations of workers that bargain as a unit with employers for a host of things, including higher wages, benefits, and better working conditions. Other organizations can accomplish similar results in other ways. For example, some membership organizations, such as the American Medical Association and the American Bar Association serve to restrict the supply of labor, driving up the wages. One way of restricting the supply of labor is by imposing rigid licensing requirements. No one can practice medicine or law, for example, without a license, so this restricts the number of people that may legally practice in these profession to those who can pass an exam, ensuring that wages will remain high.

Discrimination

Sometimes wages are affected by discrimination. Discrimination is defined as paying someone differently, or giving them different access to jobs based on their gender, race, or other work-irrelevant characteristics. It might be tempting to simply look at the average earnings of one group and compare them to those of another and conclude that any difference is due to discrimination. But this would be very incorrect. Most of the wage differential between groups can be explained by differences in education, experience, job preferences, or all three. If there are no differences between groups or individuals with respect to these, and a wide gap in wages remains, the wage differential might indeed be caused by discrimination.

SUMMARY

Although labor markets are similar to the market for other goods and services in many ways, the role of individuals and firm are reversed. In other ways, the markets are very similar, determining wages and employment levels, just as prices and quantities are determined in other markets. While demand and supply help us understand how wages are determined in a particular labor market, there are other explanations for why wages differ among markets and even within the same market. Perhaps the most important difference between labor markets and other markets, however, is that labor markets determine the well-being of individuals. The extent to which wages and employment levels are achieved (or not), determines individuals' power to realize goals and dreams, or simply survive.

Further Reading

Bauman, Y. *A Cartoon Introduction to Microeconomics*. New York: Hill and Wang Publishers, 2010.

Landsburg, S.E. *Armchair Economist: Economics and Everyday Life*. New York: The Free Press, 1993.

Levitt, S.J., and S.J. Dubner. *Freakonomics: A Rogue Economist Explains the Hidden Side of Everything*. New York: HarperCollins, 2005.

———.*Superfreakonomics: Global Cooling, Patriotic Prostitutes, and Why Suicide Bombers Should Buy Life Insurance*. New York: HarperCollins, 2009.

Milgrom, P., and J. Roberts. *Economics, Organization, and Management*. New York: Prentice Hall, 1992.

## CHAPTER 8

THE ROLE OF GOVERNMENT IN A MARKET ECONOMY

INTRODUCTION

Most of this volume has been about how markets work. Demand and supply come together in various contexts to determine price and quantity. Consumers and producers influence and are influenced by the larger market in which they find themselves. But it would be a mistake to conclude that markets operate in a vacuum. Government plays a very important role in a (predominantly) market economy, usually by enacting and implementing policies that range all the way from helping markets work more efficiently to actually being the entire market. This chapter will raise some interesting issues, such as why cows are not extinct. Back in the days of settling the West, buffalo were hunted almost to extinction, but cows have never been put on an endangered species list. Since they are used for the same things (meat, hide, milk), why were buffalo almost obliterated, while cows were never in danger? As we examine the role of government in the U.S. economy, we will answer this question.

GOVERNMENTS AND INFRASTRUCTURE

For markets to work efficiently, they need to operate in an environment that has a solid infrastructure. Government provides some of the most important components of this indispensable infrastructure, so this will be the first stop on our journey investigating the relationship between government and markets. Oddly enough, this important government function involves the least amount of government involvement in the market.

Physical Infrastructure

Imagine that a company wants to build a new manufacturing plant at the out-skirts of a city. As it constructs the new plant, it has to provide a parking lot for its employees, among other things. It does not, however, have to lay sewer lines, construct a sewage treatment facility, or build new roads that provide access to the plant. Most companies rely on governments to provide these aspects of physical infrastructure that make it possible for them to conduct business. On a broader scale, governments provide the streets, interstate highways, railway lines, and airports that businesses use to transport the goods they produce. Governments also provide police and fire protection, waste treatment facili-ties, and subsidized utilities for business use. These types of infrastructure are shared among businesses, so that no individual company has to build its own roads or hire its own firefighters. Because there is a central provider of shared infrastructure, markets can work quite efficiently. This government-provided infrastructure is also cost effective because individual companies do not have to channel their resources to building their own and can reserve their resources for achieving their direct business objectives.

Legal Infrastructure

In much the same way the government provides much of the physical infra-structure that facilitate market operations, it also provides the legal environ-ment within which businesses function. By providing various types of legal structures, government makes it possible for businesses to operate with less risk, thus improving market efficiency.

Criminal Law

On the surface, criminal law seems to be far removed from how markets oper-ate, but even laws relating to burglary guarantee that market exchanges are vol-untary. If I want what you have, you either have to give it to me or sell it to me—I cannot just take it. Therefore, having laws that prohibit involuntary exchanges help markets work more efficiently, because such laws ensure that those who place a high value on something, receive it.

Contract Law

The existence of laws that provide the framework for contracts is also very important in the efficient function of markets. Contracts allow transactions to be conducted over a period of time, rather than in one period. For example, let's assume that a wheat farmer is interested in selling his/her wheat once it is harvested. A business interested in buying the wheat wants to agree on a price with the farmer now, before the wheat is even planted, so that it knows what its production costs for flour will be. The farmer would also like to agree on a price now, before the wheat is planted, so he/she knows what income to expect for the year. So the farmer and the wheat buyer enter into a contract, an agreement to sell and buy the wheat at a future date at an agreed-upon price. If contract law did not exist, buyers and sellers would be reluctant to enter into such agreements, not knowing if they could be enforced.

Property Law

An efficient market also requires a clear process for determining property rights. Suppose, for example, that you want to buy a used car. Before you hand over any money, you would certainly expect the seller to produce the car title—proof that he/she owns the car and has a right to sell it. Without this car title, how do you know that the seller really owns the car? This is a simple example, but it can be applied to almost everything that is considered property. A clear system of property rights establishes the rights of those engaged in market transactions. Without such a system, a lot of time would be spent on trying to figure out who owns what and whether something can legally be sold by the person trying to sell it.

Antitrust Law

Antitrust laws prevent businesses from limiting competition. One way businesses in a particular industry might attempt to limit competition is by striking agreements among themselves to fix prices. Another way to limit competition might be to interfere with a rival firm's ability to fairly compete in the market. Not long ago, Microsoft was accused of attempting to monopolize the operating systems market by bundling exclusive software packages to hardware manufacturers. The government claimed this was restraint of trade because if a computer comes with software already installed, the consumer is much less likely to buy a competing brand's of software. (Why buy something your computer already has?) The government and Microsoft reached a settlement in which Microsoft agreed to stop bundling its software with computers in exclusive agreements.

Antitrust laws also come into play when two firms want to merge. If the government suspects that the merger is likely to restrict competition, it will not allow the merger to take place.

GOVERNMENTS AND INEFFICIENCIES

Up until this point, the role of government has been to support market activities, or to put some restraints on markets that do not have the ability to restrain themselves. Sometimes, however, markets simply do not produce the "right" amount--an amount that is the "socially efficient" amount. Below, we'll examine just what this means, why it occurs, and finally, what government can do about it.

Socially Efficient Quantity

In the initial discussion about demand and supply (in Chapter 2), we identified the point at which demand and supply are equal—the equilibrium point.

At this point, there is no unmet demand, there is no seller who cannot find a buyer—the quantity that consumers want is equal to the quantity that sellers want to sell. But something else is true at this point. Remember that the demand curve also represents the utility, or value that consumers place on the product. Remember, too, that the supply curve represents the marginal cost to firms of making the product. Therefore, the equilibrium point is also the point where these two things are equal. In other words, the equilibrium quantity is the quantity at which the marginal benefit, or value of that unit is exactly equal to the marginal cost of producing it.

Let's revisit the market for Bubbly Pop (Figure 8.1) and look at what the situation would be if the quantity bought and sold were 4 units. At 4 units, consumers value the last unit (the fourth) at an amount that's about $0.90. The marginal cost of producing that fourth unit is about $0.60. Consumers value this unit more than it costs producers to make it—so it should be produced and consumed.

Now let's look at the situation at 8 units. The eighth and last unit is valued by consumers at $0.50, but costs producers $1.00 to make. Therefore, this unit should not be produced and consumed. As you have surely guessed at this point, the equilibrium point of 6 units represents the point at which the cost of producing the sixth unit ($0.75) is exactly equal to the value that consumers place on this unit ($0.75). The equilibrium quantity, then, represents the point at which the "right" amount—from a societal standpoint—is being produced.

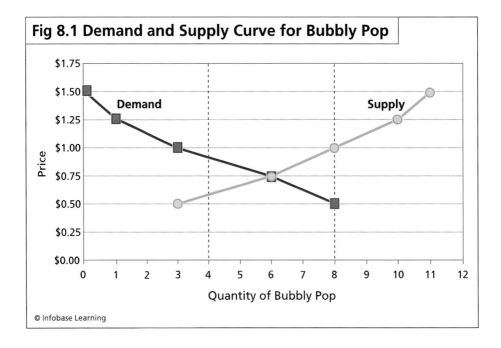

Fig 8.1 Demand and Supply Curve for Bubbly Pop

If this equilibrium, representing societal benefit and societal cost, is the "best" quantity, why would it ever be anything else? But as the examples below will reveal, exceptions can and do occur.

Negative Externalities

Negative externality may sound complex, but it basically means that those who are not part of a market exchange are harmed because of the market exchange. A couple of non-market examples illustrate this concept rather well. A negative externality could be a loud party (you are not invited, so you are not part of the exchange, but are negatively affected by it because it prevents you from sleeping). Another negative externality might be someone talking on a cell phone at a movie (you are not part of the conversation, but you are negatively affected by it because you can't hear what the actors on screen are saying). In business, negative externalities work the same way.

Let's assume that you want to buy a sweater, so you go to the mall, find one you like, and purchase it. You benefit from the purchase—no one else does. The costs incurred in the production of the sweater are borne by the manufacturer—no one else. But let's look more closely at the manufacturer. What if this company could get all its yarn for free? Would it produce more or fewer sweaters? The free yarn would lower the company's costs of doing business, so the supply curve would shift to the right, and more sweaters would be made. Now what if the producer had such a great work environment that workers wanted to work there for free? Same result, right? The quantity of sweaters produced would go up. In fact, any time that the producer can avoid a cost—any cost—that producer will increase the quantity they make.

Now let's suppose that the sweater manufacturing plant sits on the banks of a river. In the process of making sweaters, the plant generates a lot of pollution, which it spews into the river. Downriver from the plant is a recreational area that is heavily used by boaters, fishing enthusiasts, and others. The sweater firm goes about its business, taking orders, hiring workers, producing sweaters. But in the process of doing so the producer is causing harm to people who have nothing at all to do with the making of sweaters. You should recognize this as another example of a negative externality—those who are not part of the market exchange are harmed by its occurrence. The boaters on the river are not part of making sweaters at all, but they are affected when they are made. In other words, the sweater producer is generating a cost that is not borne by the company making the product but by others—everybody downstream.

The firm's private costs include the cost of raw materials, wages for workers, and equipment. But the social costs include all of these things plus the pollution that the firm generates while producing sweaters. However, the firm will produce according to its private costs—in other words, they will produce "too much"—more than the socially efficient amount. From society's standpoint, the efficient quantity would be the point where social costs equal social benefits—a smaller quantity than that produced when private costs equal social benefits.

The government has two possible options in this case. First, it can simply force the sweater business to cut back on production. Because the firm is producing too much, the government could force it to produce only the socially efficient amount. It can do this directly, by dictating the number of sweaters that may be produced, or (more likely), indirectly by regulating how much pollution the firm is permitted to generate. If the firm has to reduce the amount of pollution it generates, that means it must either reduce its production of sweaters or find a cleaner, alternative way to produce them.

The second possibility is for the government to force the firm to "internalize" the externality that it generates. The reason that the firm produces too much is that it can push a cost (the pollution) onto others. But if it had to take account of this cost in its production decisions, it would choose to produce less. The primary way the government can make this firm "feel the pain" it causes others is through taxes. This will increase the firm's private costs, making them equal to the social costs, and the firm will then produce the socially efficient amount. The government can tax the firm per unit of output (per sweater), or it can tax the pollution the firm generates. Either way results in a decrease in production.

So which is the better way to deal with this pollution problem? Should the government dictate the level of pollution, or should it provide an economic incentive to reduce pollution by taxing it? Let's compare. Say we have two polluting firms. Firm A is a low polluter. It is already operating below the level that the government wants to establish as the maximum pollution allowable in this industry. Firm B is a heavy polluter—way above the limit the government wants to establish. If the government establishes this pollution threshold, it might be in Firm A's best interest to *increase* its level of pollution to the threshold because it could save some money in doing so—the firm can actually remove whatever pollution controls it has installed. On the other hand, if the government taxes pollution, then both firms have an incentive to reduce pollution, regardless of their current pollution level.

A newer approach to controlling pollution involves the government issuing tradable pollution permits, or allowances. The government establishes a pollution threshold, then firms can buy and sell permits to exceed that threshold. If Firm A is already a low polluter, it now has an incentive to keep its pollution level low (rather than increase it) and sell the permits (that it does not need) to higher polluting firms, like Firm B. These pollution permits are bought and sold in an open market. Environmental groups have become participants in that market, buying up the pollution permits and taking them out of circulation. This action reduces the overall level of pollution because it results in fewer firms holding these allowances.

TABLE 8.1
Gains before Coase Solution

	Without Filter	With Filter
Gain to Ben	$130/day	$100/day
Gain to Jerry	$50/day	$100/day
Total Gain	$180/day	$200/day

Coase Solution

Is there another way that pollution can be reduced—a way that does not depend on government involvement? Under a certain set of conditions—yes. Let's assume we have two people: Ben and Jerry. Ben's factory pollutes, spewing toxic waste into the water. Jerry is a fisherman whose business is harmed by Ben's pollution. If Ben were to filter his waste water before dumping it, Jerry would incur less harm, but this option would cost Ben money. Both options, with profits per day indicated, are shown in Table 8.1.

Left to his own devices, would Ben install the filter? His daily profit without the filter is $130, whereas his profit with the filter is $100. He would not install the filter even though Jerry would gain ($50/day compared to $100/day) and it would be the socially optimal result ($180/day compared to $200/day) if he did. The only thing Ben is considering in making this decision is his own cost, and the filter would cost him $30 a day.

Is it necessary for the government to get involved in this situation? The answer is No. Notice that the cost of the filter ($30) is less than the gain to Jerry ($50). Therefore, Jerry has an incentive to pay Ben for the cost of the filter, and

TABLE 8.2
Gains after Coase Solution

	Without Filter	With Filter
Gain to Ben	$130/day	$140/day
Gain to Jerry	$50/day	$60/day
Total Gain	$180/day	$200/day

both would be better off. Table 8.2 shows what would happen if Jerry went to Ben and offered him $40 a day to install the filter.

The profits without the filter do not change, but Ben's profit with the filter is $140 per day (it costs him $30, but he's getting $40 from Jerry). Jerry's profits go up with the installation of the filter, not to $100 (because he has to pay $40 to Ben) but to $60 ($100-$40). Both of them are better off with a filter rather than with no filter. This arrangement is called a **Coase solution**, named after Ronald Coase, who was awarded the Nobel Prize in Economics in 1991. When parties to a transaction of this kind can communicate and conduct their transaction in a way that costs them nothing, a private solution can be achieved, making government involvement unnecessary.

Coase solutions are easier to implement when the number of participants is small; they become harder and harder to achieve as the number of participants grows. Going back to our sweater example, it would be very difficult for all the users of the recreational area to get together, decide on a payment, and go to the sweater business with a proposal to reduce pollution. When a larger number of participants is involved, the government must step in and manage the level of pollution.

Positive Externalities

Like a negative externality, a **positive externality** occurs when someone besides those involved in a market exchange is affected by that exchange—except in a positive way. For example, when your neighbors plant a garden or paint their house, they benefit from an exchange because they received services (from a painter) and goods (from the store where they bought the plants) that they wanted. But other people living on the street also benefit because the freshly painted house and plants are attractive and make the entire neighborhood look better. Thus, everyone benefits, even those who are not part of the original exchange.

But as you saw in the discussion of negative externalities, sometimes the wrong amount of something is produced. Let's look at what can happen with education. When you decide how much education to acquire, you make that decision based upon what is best for you—how much benefit you will get from a certain level of additional education versus how much it costs to get it. But, when you become better educated, you aren't the only one who benefits. The more education you have, the higher your income is likely to be, the more taxes you will pay, and the less likely you will be to engage in criminal activities— all of these things benefit society. So your getting a good education produces a positive externality. In other words, the societal benefit is greater than your personal benefit. But when you think about how much education to get, you equate your private benefit with your private costs and choose quantity on that basis. The fact that there is a larger, societal benefit means that you are choosing an amount that is too small. In fact, from society's standpoint, you should get more education, but you do not take that into consideration. Parallel to the case of negative externality where too much is produced, with a positive externality, too little is consumed.

Here, as with the sweater factory, we will look at government's potential role in getting you to consume more so that society gets greater benefits. How can the government encourage you to consume more education? By subsidizing it. A government **subsidy** is the opposite of a tax. Instead of the government taking away money for certain activities, the government provides money for those activities. Public elementary and secondary schools are subsidized (100 percent) by the government; public college tuition is subsidized by student loans and tax revenues. For education (or research) in certain fields, specifically those areas of study or research that might produce innovations that provide additional important benefits to society, the government sometimes gives a form of subsidy called a grant. Another example of government subsidy of a market with positive externalities is the market for vaccinations. The government subsidizes the distribution of vaccines because everyone benefits when individuals are immunized.

GOVERNMENTS AND THE PROVISION OF GOODS AND SERVICES

Markets are generally efficient, but there are times (as in the case of negative and positive externalities) that they fail to produce the socially optimal quantity of some desirable good or service. In such cases, the government intervenes to promote and achieve a more socially desirable outcome. Sometimes government has a greater role—to create markets that would not exist at all if the government did not step in and provide one.

To see why there are some goods and services that markets simply will not provide, we need to divide goods and services into four categories.

Rival vs. Nonrival

The first way to divide goods is by whether they are rival or nonrival goods. **Rival goods** are those that only one person can consume. For example, if you eat a candy bar, your sister cannot eat the same one. **Nonrival goods** are those that more than one person can consume at the same time. For example, many people can watch a movie at the same time—the fact that you are watching in no way means that someone else cannot also watch it.

Excludable vs. Nonexcludable

The second way to look at goods is whether you can be prevented from consuming them or not. An **excludable good** is one that you can be prevented from consuming if you do not pay for it. The candy bar in the previous example is an excludable good—if you do not pay for it, you do not get it. A **nonexcludable**

TABLE 8.3
Types of Goods

	Rival	Nonrival
Excludable	Private goods	Quasi-public goods
Nonexcludable	Common goods	Pure public goods

good is one that you can consume even if you do not pay for it. Have you ever gone to a museum where there was no admission charge but instead, there was a donation box? That's a nonexcludable good because you can enjoy the museum without having to pay (although they certainly would like it if you did).

Table 8.3 presents the four combinations of goods and services. First, let's look at rival, excludable goods. These are goods that can be consumed by only one person at a time, and can be consumed only if they are paid for. Probably most of the goods and services you consume throughout your day are private goods. The market provides these goods, although the government may become involved if there is a need to ensure fair competition or to address market failures.

Next, let's look at nonrival, excludable goods. These are goods that more than one person can consume at a time, but only in exchange for payment. Going to the movies is an example of a quasi-public good, as is pay-per-view. You can invite a hundred of your friends to your house to watch a boxing match on pay-per-view, so all of you can consume it at the same time. But as "pay-per-view" suggests, someone has to pay for it. Going to a national park is another example. Many people can visit the park at the same time, but every visitor has to pay to get in.

Nonexcludable, rival goods are goods that do not have to be paid for, but only one person can consume them at a time. For example, if you catch a fish, I cannot catch the same fish (rival), but we do not have to pay anything for catching the fish (we do not have to pay per fish, although we might have to pay for a license). These kinds of goods are called common goods, after the example, the Tragedy of the Commons. People in agricultural societies lived in villages and often shared a common, open grassland used for grazing animals. No one owned the grassland—it was shared by everyone, so it was called "the common" and was nonexcludable. It was, however, rival because the grass that one person's sheep ate could not be eaten by another person's sheep. The problem with shared resources such as this grassland, is that they tend to be overused.

Because no one owned this resource (i.e., the commons) no one could be prevented from using it, and they quickly became depleted. Hence the tragedy.

Finally, let's look at public goods. These are goods that more than one person can consume at a time, and no one can be prevented from consuming, with or without payment. And it is precisely this combination of characteristics that ensures that no private market will provide these goods. If I can enjoy a good or service whether I pay for it or not, and thousands or millions of other people can also consume it at the same time without paying a cent, there is no profit incentive for a private firm to provide that good or service. Real-life examples are easy to find. For example, everyone is protected by the police whether paying for this protection or not. Taxes pay for police protection, but even those who do not pay taxes (the homeless, for example), are entitled to police protection. If someone receives the service without paying for it, economists call this free riding. There is no private market for police protection because those who do not pay are also covered. Obviously, there is no opportunity for profit in such cases and because the goal of markets is profit, markets do not provide these goods and service—public goods and services are provided by government.

Are you ready to answer our question that opened this chapter—why did buffalo almost become extinct when cows did not? They were used for the same purposes, but they had one very critical difference. Cows were private property; the buffalo were not owned by anyone—they were a common good. And like all common goods, the risk of overuse is real. So much so, that they were almost overused into extinction.

SUMMARY

Government has several important roles within market economies. It provides the physical and legal infrastructures that allow markets to operate and ensure they work smoothly and efficiently. The government also can increase market efficiency when it encourages competition and prevents markets from getting too big. Sometimes markets, when left to their own devices, produce the wrong amounts from a social efficiency standpoint. If there are negative or positive externalities, efficiency is increased when the government intervenes to move the market toward a socially optimal quantity. Finally, in the case of public goods and services, the government is the sole provider because public goods and services earn no profits and markets are not interested in producing or offering them.

Further Reading

Arnold, R.A. *How to Think Like an Economist*. Mason, Ohio: South-Western College Publishing, 2004.

Bauman, Y. *A Cartoon Introduction to Microeconomics*. New York: Hill and Wang Publishers, 2010.

Landsburg, S.E. *Armchair Economist: Economics and Everyday Life*. New York: The Free Press, 1993.

Levitt, S.J., and S.J. Dubner. *Freakonomics: A Rogue Economist Explains the Hidden Side of Everything*. New York: HarperCollins, 2005.

———. *Superfreakonomics: Global Cooling, Patriotic Prostitutes, and Why Suicide Bombers Should Buy Life Insurance*. New York: HarperCollins, 2009.

Miller, R.L., D.K. Benjamin, and D.C. North. *Economics of Public Issues*, New York: Pearson, 2012.

GLOSSARY

above-normal return   Profit that is more than both explicit costs and opportunity costs.

adverse selection   When one side of the market has more information than the other side and uses this information to its advantage.

capital   Plant and equipment in a production process.

cartel   A group of producers that come together to restrict output and/or control price.

change in demand   A shift of the demand curve, caused by a change in income, prices of related goods, population, expectations, or tastes and preferences.

change in quantity demanded   A movement along a given demand curve, caused by a change in price.

change in quantity supplied   A movement along a given supply curve, caused by a change in price.

change in supply   A shift of the supply curve, caused by a change in input prices, technology, expectations, or the number of firms.

Coase solution   A situation where a limited number of participants can come to an agreement in the presence of negative externalities, resulting in an efficient market outcome without the need for government action.

collusion   The act of producers explicitly agreeing on production quotas or market prices; it is illegal in the United States.

common goods   Rival, nonexcludable goods; no private ownership promotes overuse.

compensating wage differential Either the increase in wage needed to induce a worker to work in an unpleasant or risky job or the decrease in wage paid to a worker who works at a job offering certain amenities.

complement A good that is consumed together with another good.

constant returns to scale A situation in which a firm increases its inputs by some factor and output goes up by the same factor.

cross-price elasticity A measure of the responsiveness of the quantity of one good when another good's price changes.

decreasing returns to scale A situation in which a firm increases its inputs by a factor and output increases by less than that factor.

derived demand Labor demand that depends upon the demand of a firm's output.

diminishing marginal benefit Where the additional benefit of an action falls the more the action is performed.

diminishing marginal product As workers are hired, the last worker will contribute less to output than the worker before.

diminishing returns to labor See diminishing marginal product.

discrimination Restricting access (to employment, education, housing, etc.) on the basis of an unrelated characteristic, such as race, gender, ethnicity, or religion.

diseconomies of scale What occurs when a firm increases its inputs by a given factor and output increases by less than that factor.

dominant strategy The best course of action for a firm (or individual), regardless of what the other firm (or individual) does.

economic profit A profit that covers explicit costs and opportunity costs.

economies of scale What occurs when a firm increases its inputs by a factor and output increases by more than that factor.

elastic A characteristic of demand, where consumers are very responsive to price changes.

elasticity A measure of consumer responsiveness to price changes.

equilibrium The price and quantity determined when demand is equal to supply.

equilibrium price (market clearing price) The price at which demand is equal to supply.

excise tax A tax placed on each unit of good sold.

excludable goods Goods that individuals can be prevented from consuming if they do not pay for them.

explicit cost   A direct cost of production, which must be paid with money.

fixed cost   A cost that does not change with the amount of output produced.

fixed input   A resource that does not change in the short run.

free riding   A situation in which an individual can enjoy the benefits of a good or service without having to pay for it.

game theory   A subfield of economics that analyzes oligopolistic markets.

human capital   The investments that individuals make in themselves to increase their productivity.

implicit cost   Opportunity cost, or the value of the next best alternative.

income elasticity   A measure of how responsive individuals are in their consumption of a good when their incomes change.

increasing returns to scale   What occurs when a firm increases its inputs by a given factor and output increases by more than that factor.

inelastic   A description of demand in which the quantity consumers demand does not change very much when price changes.

inferior good   A good that consumers want less of when their income increases; or a good that consumers want more of when their income decreases.

input   A resource used by firm to produce an output.

law of demand   The observation that when the price of a good falls, quantity demanded increases.

law of diminishing marginal utility   As more units are consumed, the additional satisfaction from each additional unit falls.

law of supply   The observation that when the price of a good falls, firms provide less of that good to the market.

long run   A period of time during which all inputs are variable.

macroeconomics   The study of the economy as a whole, a "big picture" approach.

marginal benefit   The additional benefit from consuming one more unit.

marginal cost   The additional cost to the firm of producing one more unit.

marginal product of labor   The additional output produced by one more worker.

marginal revenue product   The value of the output produced by one more worker.

marginal utility   The additional satisfaction to a consumer from consuming one more unit.

market   When buyers and sellers come together to exchange goods and services.

market power   A firm's ability to affect the market price.

microeconomics   The study of how individuals and firms make decisions.

monopolistic competition   A market structure with many buyers and sellers, no barriers to entry or exit, and products that are only slightly different from each other.

monopoly   A market structure with only one seller of a good with no close substitutes.

mutually beneficial exchange   When both parties to a transaction gain from it.

negative externality   A situation in which individuals who are not part of a market exchange are harmed by the exchange.

nonexcludable goods   Goods that individuals cannot be prevented from consuming, even if they do not pay for them.

nonrival goods   Goods that more than one person can consume at a time.

normal good   A good that consumers want more of if their incomes increase; a good that consumers want less of if their incomes decrease.

normal return   A profit that covers only explicit and opportunity costs.

oligopoly   A market structure with just a few firms that make interdependent decisions.

opportunity cost   The next best alternative; the cost of the choice not made.

output   What a firm produces.

perfect competition   A market structure with many buyers and sellers, no barriers to entry, and identical products.

positive externality   A situation in which individuals who are not a part of a market exchange benefit from the exchange.

price ceiling   A maximum price that can be charged in a market.

price floor   A minimum price that can be charged in a market.

price support   See price floor.

Prisoner's dilemma   A two-person decision-making situation in which the parties choose an outcome that is not in their joint best interests.

profit   Total revenue minus total costs.

reservation wage   The minimum wage at which an individual is willing to work.

rival goods   Goods that only one person can consume at a time.

scale   The size of a firm, or the level of capital.

short run   A period of time during which some resources are fixed.

subsidy   A government payment that encourages and/or supports some activity.

substitute   A good that consumers choose instead of another good.

sunk costs   Costs that occurred in the past and cannot be recovered.

total revenue   Money received from selling a product; it is computed by multiplying price by quantity.

total utility   The total amount of satisfaction obtained from consuming something.

variable cost   Costs that change with the level of production.

variable input   An input into the production process that can change in the short run.

BIBLIOGRAPHY

Ariely, D. *Predictably Irrational: The Hidden Forces That Shape Our Decisions.* New York: HarperCollins, 2008.

———. *The Upside of Irrationality: The Unexpected Benefits of Defying Logic and Work and at Home.* New York: HarperCollins, 2010.

Arnold, R.A. *How to Think Like an Economist.* Mason, Ohio: South-Western College Publishing, 2004.

Bauman, Y. *A Cartoon Introduction to Microeconomics.* New York: Hill and Wang Publishers, 2010.

Colander, D. *Microeconomics.* New York: McGraw-Hill, 2008. New York, New York.

———. Colander, D. *The Stories Economists Tell.* New York: McGraw-Hill, 2005.

Frank, R.H. *Microeconomics and Behavior.* New York: McGraw-Hill, 2009.

Hall, R.E., and M. Lieberman. *Microeconomics: Principles and Applications.* Mason, Ohio: South-Western Cengage Learning, 2010.

Harford, T. *The Logic of Life: The Rational Economics of an Irrational World.* New York: Random House, 2009.

———. *The Undercover Economist.* New York: Random House, 2007.

Heyne, P., P.J. Boettke, and D.L. Prychitko. *The Economic Way of Thinking.* New York: Prentice Hall, 2009.

Hubbard, R.G., and A.P. O'Brien. *Microeconomics.* Upper Saddle River, N.J.: Pearson Education, 2008.

Jevons, M. *A Deadly Indifference: A Henry Spearman Mystery*. Princeton, N.J.: Princeton University Press, 1995.

———. *Fatal Equilibrium*. Greenwich, Conn.: Fawcett Publishing, 1986.

———. *Murder at the Margin*. Princeton, N.J.: Princeton University Press, 1993.

Krugman, P., and R. Wells. *Microeconomics*. New York: Worth Publishers, 2008.

Landsburg, S.E. *Armchair Economist: Economics and Everyday Life*. New York: The Free Press, 1993.

Levitt, S.J., and S.J. Dubner. *Freakonomics: A Rogue Economist Explains the Hidden Side of Everything*. New York: HarperCollins, 2005.

———. *Superfreakonomics: Global Cooling, Patriotic Prostitutes, and Why Suicide Bombers Should Buy Life Insurance*. New York: HarperCollins, 2009.

Lindstrom, M. *Buyology: Truth and Lies About Why We Buy*. New York: Random House, 2008.

Mankiw, N.G. *Principles of Microeconomics*. Mason, Ohio: South-Western, Cengage Learning, 2012.

Milgrom, P., and J. Roberts, J. *Economics, Organization, and Management*. New York: Prentice Hall, 1992.

Poundstone, W. *Prisoner's Dilemma*. New York: Doubleday, 1992.

Rosenthal, E.C. *The Complete Idiot's Guide to Game Theory*. New York: Penguin Group, 2011.

Schwartz, B. *The Paradox of Choice: Why More Is Less*. New York: HarperCollins, 2004.

Thaler, R.H., and C.R. Sunstein. *Nudge: Improving Decisions About Health, Wealth and Happiness*. New Haven, Conn.: Yale University Press, 2008.

Wheelan, C. *The Naked Economics: Undressing the Dismal Science*. New York: W. W. Norton, 2009.

INDEX

Index note: Page numbers followed by *g* indicate glossary entries.

H

happiness 59. *See also* utility
human capital 121–123, 139*g*

I

immigrant labor 119
implicit cost 68, 139*g. See also* opportunity cost(s)
income changes
    and change in demand 17, 18–19, 31, 54–56
    and equilibrium 31
    and income elasticity 54–56
income elasticity 54–56, 139*g*
increasing returns to scale 79–80, 139*g*
inefficiencies, social 127–133
inelastic demand 43, 139*g*
    on demand curve 50, 51
    for necessities 46–47
    and substitutes 48
    and total revenue 43–44, 45
inferior goods 19, 139*g*
    demand for 18–19, 54, 55–56
information, asymmetry of 6–8
infrastructure 125–127
    legal 126–127
    physical 126
innovation
    and change in supply 28
    and demand for labor 117
    government grants for 133
    government protections for 97–98
    in monopoly 106
    in oligopoly 97–98
    patents for 97–98, 106
input(s) 67, 139*g*
    control over 98
    fixed 67–68, 69, 70, 73, 139*g*
    in long run 78–80
    price increases for 26–27, 31–32
    scale of, deciding 78–80
    in short run 67–68, 69, 78–79
    variable 68, 69, 141*g*

L

labor
    demand curve for 113, 114
        shifts in 115–117, 120, 121
    demand for 109–117
        changes in 120, 121
        factors affecting 115–117
    as input 67, 68, 69, 70–71
    marginal product of (MP) 70–73, 110–111, 139*g*
        changes in 116–117
        diminishing 72–73, 77–78, 138*g*

price of. *See* wage(s)
productivity of. *See* worker productivity
specialization of 71, 72, 73, 112–113
supply curve of 118, 119
supply of 118–119
    changes in 119, 120–121
    restrictions on 124
labor/capital mix 69
labor market 109–124
    demand in 109–117, 120, 121
    equilibrium in 120–121
    v. other markets 109–110
    supply in 118–119, 120–121, 124
law(s)
    antitrust 127
    contract 126–127
    criminal 126
    of demand 16–17, 139*g*
    of diminishing marginal utility 61–62, 65, 139*g*
    immigration 119
    property 127
    of supply 25, 139*g*
    on transplant organ sales 37
law practice 124
legal infrastructure 126–127
leisure, opportunity cost of 118
licensing requirements 124
long run 68, 78–80, 139*g*
luxury tax 57

M

macroeconomics
    definition of 139*g*
    v. microeconomics 3–4
Manning, Peyton 123
marginal benefit 10–12, 139*g*
    diminishing 10–11, 138*g*
marginal costs (MC)
    in decision making 11–12
    of labor, wage as 113
    of production 76–78, 139*g*
    in profit maximization calculation 86
marginal decision making 9–12
marginal product of labor (MP) 70–73, 110–111, 139*g*
    changes in 116–117
    diminishing 72–73, 77–78, 138*g*
marginal revenue 84–86
    for labor 113
    in monopoly 104, 105
    in perfect competition
        for firm 88–90, 91, 92
        for market 88
marginal revenue product (MRP) 111–114, 139*g*